改善

THE

SPIRIT OF

KAIZEN

Creating Lasting Excellence
One Small Step at a Time

Robert Maurer, Ph.D.

New York   Chicago   San Francisco   Lisbon   London
Madrid   Mexico City   Milan   New Delhi   San Juan
Seoul   Singapore   Sydney   Toronto

*The **McGraw·Hill** Companies*

2 3 4 5 6 7 8 9 0   QFR/QFR   1 8 7 6

ISBN: 978-0-07-179617-0
MHID: 0-07-179617-7

e-ISBN: 978-0-07-179618-7
e-MHID: 0-07-179618-5

This publication is designed to provide accurate and authoritative information in regard to the subject matter covered. It is sold with the understanding that neither the author nor the publisher is engaged in rendering legal, accounting, or other professional service. If legal advice or other expert assistance is required, the services of a competent professional person should be sought.

—From a Declaration of Principles Jointly Adopted by a Committee of the American Bar Association and a Committee of Publishers and Associations

McGraw-Hill books are available at special quantity discounts to use as premiums and sales promotions, or for use in corporate training programs. To contact a representative, please e-mail us at bulksales@mcgraw-hill.com.

This book is printed on acid-free paper.

For Ben and John Sikorra,

the bravest men I have ever known,

and for their amazing parents,

Lori and Joe

CONTENTS

Contents

改

ACKNOWLEDGMENTS

This book is the work of many people, and I am grateful to have the opportunity to share their wisdom and talents with you. Leigh Ann Hirschman, my cowriter, put lyrics and melody to these kaizen concepts. Jennifer Griffin, my agent, provided encouragement and enthusiasm for the project. My father, Mort Maurer, demonstrated the power of kaizen and the importance of creativity through his lifetime of experience and success in many business enterprises. Knox Huston, senior editor at McGraw-Hill, guided this book to publication. My friend Steve Albert's humor and love have always kept me from taking myself too seriously.

Finally, I'd like to offer much appreciation for my family: Dia, Larry, and Dru. Thank you for sharing my passion for this project.

Chapter One

A SWIFT INTRODUCTION TO KAIZEN

Business culture loves the idea of revolutionary, immediate change. But turnaround efforts often fail because radical change sets off our brain's fear response and shuts down our powers to think clearly and creatively. A more effective path to change begins with the small steps of kaizen. *These quiet steps bypass our mental alarm system, allowing our creative and intellectual processes to flow without obstruction. The result: Change that is both lasting and powerful.*

Leaders are often called upon to make significant improvements to their organizations—to cut costs, to create new products, to reduce mistakes, to improve service, and so on. It is possible to make these improvements by gritting your teeth, squaring your shoulders, and forging ahead no matter what the obstacles.

改

2

Possible, but not likely. Some managers enjoy this kind of bareknuckled attack on their organization's problems, and a few even succeed at it. Their stories are dramatic ("I led our team through a complete reorganization in six months!") and feature admirable determination ("I was poor and uneducated, but I didn't let anything stand in my way; now I'm the head of my own multibillion-dollar business!"), so they are the ones that draw our attention. If you absorb enough of these stories, you can easily get the impression that the only way to reach your management goals is to hurtle yourself at them, tearing down the fast track to success at breakneck speed and obliterating all barriers in your path. You can also draw the conclusion that if you haven't reached your goals, the reason must be that you're lacking in skill or good old-fashioned grit.

Not so. Most of us are programmed to resist radical change. Let me say that again: *We are built to resist radical change.* As you'll see in the coming pages, our nervous system wires us for resistance to a big overhaul of any kind. This truth applies not just to managers but also to the employees we need to carry out our programs for change. So if you've tried to change your organization and met with disappointment, there is no reason to feel guilty.

But there *is* reason to feel optimistic. Most groups can achieve success when they step off the fast track and take an alternative path. This path is soft underfoot and shaded overhead. It's such an unassuming little byway that it doesn't attract the world's notice, but believe me, some of the most successful people and organizations have been using it for decades with consistently good results. This path starts with the smallest of steps. It causes no stress, no fear . . . and you can take it all the way to your goal.

But before I tell you more about kaizen, I'd like you to meet some struggling business owners.

"WE NEED SOMETHING BOLD AND INNOVATIVE!"

At the time this story began, I was a clinical professor at the University of California, Los Angeles (UCLA) School of Medicine; I specialized in teaching behavioral health. It was not long past graduation, and many of our students had been hired by existing physician groups or had banded together to start large groups of their own. Four of the doctors, however, had decided to create a small private practice devoted to family medicine. They were deliberate about this decision. They wanted to give their patients thoughtful, personal care, and they worried that their freedom to practice as they wished would be stifled by joining a bigger group.

When the practice opened, I called to congratulate the young doctors on their new business. However, the voices on the other end of the conversation sounded far from celebratory. They were in trouble, they explained. They'd committed to a lease on a beautiful office in a prime Santa Monica location and had taken on heavy debt to pay for state-of-the-art equipment. In addition, each doctor had his or her own student debts to pay off. All of these obligations would have been manageable, they said, with a steady flow of patients. But the patients weren't coming. Their city, Santa Monica, had more than its share of doctors, and my former students were realizing that they had entered a very competitive business world, one that their medical training hadn't prepared them for. Although they were bright, focused, and creative, they were also terrified of losing everything.

Sensing their distress, business consultants were knocking on the practice door, offering them assistance and assurances of future prosperity—at a steep price. The doctors were trying to figure out where to get the money to hire one of these consultants, or maybe a public-relations expert. One physician partner, with strain cracking her voice, was arguing to take on more debt. "If we want to win big," she insisted, "we have to play big. We need something bold and innovative to drive patients to our doors." Yet she, like the others, was unable to come up with a specific idea that might work.

I sympathized. These were good, caring doctors who could bring excellent care to their community. I wanted them to feel hopeful and creative again. But the one thing I didn't want them to do was to try to innovate their way out of the problem.

INNOVATION WORKS, EXCEPT WHEN IT DOESN'T

Why not? What's wrong with innovation?

First, here's a definition. Sometimes the word *innovation* is used to refer to a new idea or a clever solution, but in this book I'll adhere to the meaning that's taught in business schools. There, *innovation* means change, but not just any kind of change; innovation is a dramatic, sweeping change, one that's usually undertaken in a short amount of time. Innovation can be a clearly positive, exciting change, such as the Apple computer's marriage of scientific function and elegant design. Or innovation can be a much more difficult change, like an austerity program that lays off thousands of workers.

Other examples of innovation include:

- Changing the focus of your organization
- Adapting a never-before-used technology.
- Hiring all new department heads.
- Declaring bankruptcy.
- Merging with another company.
- Transforming the company's image.

When innovation goes well, the result is new products, creative solutions to old problems, and vigorous organizations. And it's fast! If you know you can you achieve a goal quickly, why not wait a minute longer than you have to?

The problem isn't with innovation itself. It's with our single-minded approach to innovation. When we believe that radical change—the fast track—is the *only* path to survival, growth, and ingenuity, we lose some of our effectiveness. If we think that wrenching change is the sole solution to problems, well . . . we tend to let those problems go for a long time. A major overhaul can feel too hard, too painful, and too time-consuming to manage, especially when we have so many other things to do. And so the problem grows. When the problem is too big to ignore, we finally decide to do something about it . . . and charge fiercely toward a solution. We say, "Let's turn this culture around!" Or "We're going to do the impossible around here!" If we succeed, that's terrific.

改

But when change tears through an organization, managers and staff may not feel as invigorated as you'd like them to. They often freeze up or feel overwhelmed. That's a big problem because radical change usually involves radical risk: a huge investment of money, time, people, or goodwill. When radical change fails, it can take down an entire department or even a whole organization. The difficulty of sustaining an innovative approach to change is the story of NASA in the 1990s, and of Ford and Xerox at the turn of the millennium; these are all examples of organizations that tried innovation and were left weakened and on their knees. You can probably think of examples from your own experience: breakneck deadlines that resulted in sloppy, slapped-together products, morale initiatives that caused skepticism and scorn, and demands for creativity that led to stalled-out groupthink.

That's why I didn't want the family-medicine group to turn to innovation. They were already feeling scared and overwhelmed. With their emotional resources depleted, they were in a weak position to carry out any kind of radical change. They also lacked the money to revamp their practice. I hated to see them dig deeper into debt with such unsure results.

Kaizen and Innovation: Two Strategies for Change

改善

When you need to make a change, there are two basic strategies you can use: innovation and kaizen. Innovation calls for a radical, immediate rethink of the status quo. Kaizen, on the other hand, asks for nothing other than small, doable steps toward improvement.

善

7

Fortunately innovation is not the only way to create change. There's an alternative, one that it is so simple and painless that people tend to dismiss it. Yet this method is extremely effective, whether you want to make a small adjustment to your staff or transform the globe. And all you have to do is take one small—very small—step at a time.

KAIZEN: GOOD CHANGE

I'm talking, of course, about kaizen. *Kaizen* is a term from the Japanese language. It's a wonderfully perfect word that literally means "good change." The Asian origins of the word are a little bit misleading, though, because you can easily get the impression that kaizen is at its core a uniquely

Japanese philosophy, one that might be difficult to translate into Western culture. Actually, kaizen was born in the United States during World War II, a time that drew out the very best qualities in Americans—our imagination, our bravery, and our willingness to work shoulder-to-shoulder to get the job done.

When France fell to Nazi Germany in 1940, the American government realized that it would need to supply the Allied nations with arms, ammunition, food, and equipment. The speedy conversion of factories from producers of domestic goods to producers of wartime material was a heady challenge in itself. Then the United States entered the war. Just when we needed minds and hands to produce supplies, many of our best managers and workers were leaving for overseas combat. It was a grave situation. We needed soldiers to fight the Axis powers, but without guns and tanks, those soldiers would be fighting in vain.

In response, the U.S. government created a series of programs called Training Within Industry (TWI), which taught corporations how to become more efficient and more productive. One of TWI's most important insights was that companies needed to resist the impulse to perform a total makeover. "There isn't time," counseled the TWI course manual. "Don't try to plan a whole new department layout or go after a big new installation of new equipment." Instead, TWI experts offered a philosophy you've probably heard before: *continuous improvement.* "Look for hundreds of small things you can improve," they advised. "Look for improvements on existing jobs with your present equipment." The experts were insistent that supervisors pay respectful attention to every

改

employee, viewing each one as a potential source of ideas, information, and suggestions.

Pay attention to employees. Look for small improvements. Make do with what you have. It doesn't seem like much of a management philosophy, especially not when lives and nations were on the line. Yet historians will tell you that the small steps of TWI worked. A significant reason for the Allied victory in World War II was the United States' ability to produce high-quality, reliable equipment and to get that equipment overseas quickly. When the war ended, however, so did TWI. Former soldiers took up their old places in the manufacturing sector, and they brought back their old, pre-war habits of work with them. Business settled back down to normal, and continuous improvement was left behind.

善

In Japan, however, business was anything but normal. Not only had it suffered the loss of life and morale that went with its wartime defeat, Japan's industries were decimated. The U.S. government had an interest in improving Japan's economy, reasoning that a strong Japan would act as a buffer between the United States and North Korea. To that end, the United States provided management-training courses to Japanese businesses. One of the advisors to Japanese industries at this time was an American statistician named W. (William) Edwards Deming. Dr. Deming had been instrumental in formulating assistance to American businesses during the war. Now he took his ideas—about continuous improvement, small steps toward progress, reduction of waste, respect for workers, and service to the customer—to the Japanese leaders. They paid very close attention, and the rest is history. Based on the small-step philosophy that it came to call "kaizen," Japanese businesses rose to dominance in the second half of the twentieth century.

In 1980, American businesses were increasingly nervous about the competition they faced from an efficient, energetic, quality-driven Japan. NBC ran a special on the television show *NBC White Paper* called "If Japan Can . . . Why Can't We?" featuring W. Edwards Deming and his ideas. Dr. Deming became a wildly popular consultant and speaker in the United States, whose businesses once again listened to his suggestions for continuous improvement. Kaizen was embraced by many U.S. businesses, mostly as a highly technical production and operations concept. In the United States, kaizen lives today through practices that include lean production, just-in-time (JIT) delivery, and statistical control of processes.

THIS IS NOT YOUR B-SCHOOL KAIZEN

The application of kaizen to operations has been a terrific advancement for businesses. It has reduced production waste, increased quality, and encouraged frontline workers to contribute suggestions and ideas, not just go through the motions. Along the way, however, we've missed something. We've missed the opportunity to apply kaizen to management and use it as a psychological tool for solving problems and fostering good change.

I've spent my career as a psychologist studying the mechanisms of success. In both my consulting work and as a faculty member at the UCLA and the University of

Washington medical schools, I help people who are wrestling with the problems of change. I teach them:

- How to make successful changes in their own lives.
- How to help other people change.
- How to manage the fear that comes with change.

In particular, I've seen plenty of businesspeople who need to create change. Improving quality is a perennial management concern. How, my clients wonder, can I get staff to care more, to make fewer mistakes, to waste less, and/or to attend to the details? Clients may need to confront employees whose rotten attitude is polluting the office environment. They may face crushingly tight budgets. They may need to inspire their staff to develop better products and services. Increasingly, managers also may have to become health gurus and find ways to hold down health-care costs—even if that means getting their employees to eat better and exercise more. If you are a manager of any kind, there's a lot coming down on your shoulders.

When I work with managers and executives, it's often because they've tried innovation and it hasn't succeeded. Sometimes they consult with me because they are looking for a fresh way to solve their problems. Sometimes they consult with me because the burden—all those demands on their shoulders—and that feeling of having failed is giving them physical symptoms such as backaches, headaches, insomnia, and other forms of malaise.

What I offer these clients is kaizen for managers: small, tiny steps toward improvement, some of which lead to surprisingly large-scale changes. And this is what I suggested to the young doctors, discussed earlier in this chapter, who told me about their troubles. As former students of mine, they'd heard about applying kaizen to health problems, and they'd seen their patients benefit from small steps such as exercising just one minute a day. (I know exercising for one minute a day sounds crazy, but it's effective. I'll talk about kaizen for health later in the book, in Chapter 7, "Reduce Health-Care Expenses.") But they couldn't imagine applying kaizen to their business problems, especially when those problems seemed so big. "Let me come to your office for one hour," I said, "and I'll give you a free talk about kaizen for business."

The doctors and their staff spent their lunch break one afternoon listening to the kaizen strategies that I'll outline in this book. The staff members—the nurses, receptionists, and back-office and billing personnel—caught on right away. Kaizen invites every member of an organization to contribute, and the employees liked the idea of being part of a solution. The doctors were less sure. They worried that small steps would take too long; their debts were mounting and there wasn't a lot of time. Near the end of the meeting, I divided the audience into groups of three, with a doctor, a nurse or receptionist, and a back-office worker in each. I asked each group to think of the smallest step possible that could improve the practice. There were two rules:

1. Because resources were in short supply, the step could not cost anything.

2. The idea had to benefit the customer (the patient).

One nurse immediately offered a suggestion. A few weeks previously, she'd taken her car in for service at the dealership. The next day, the dealer's service representative called to see if she was pleased with the cost, service, and results. The nurse said, "Why not introduce this level of customer service to our practice? The doctors aren't that busy right now. They can call their patients the day after the office visit. When the practice gets busier, we can all help make the calls."

The suggestion followed the two rules, and the group was willing to try it, although the doctors remained skeptical that such a small step had the power to ignite their business. But patients were surprised and delighted by the small extra attention. Word quickly spread about these new doctors in town and how well they treated their "customers." New patients began to call for appointments, and they in turn recommended friends to the practice.

As the practice grew, the office continued to rely on kaizen to solve problems. One nurse, noticing that patient complaints appeared in an inverse proportion to the time a patient spent with a doctor, suggested that doctors dictate their notes *during* the visit instead of after. It took about the same amount of time as dictating the notes at the end of the day (the custom of most doctors), but it would give the doctor more face time with the patients. The patients loved it. When they saw the doctor carefully and thoroughly summarizing their appointment, the patients felt cared for. They also had the chance to offer clarifying information or ask questions.

Later, a receptionist listened to a doctor griping about the percentage of no-shows each day. No-shows are a common problem in medical offices; even with reminder calls, the average national no-show rate is 15 percent. The receptionist mulled things over, thinking about how no-shows wasted the precious resource of medical care. She wondered if the no-shows made the connection between their actions and the effects on everyone else. She then placed a sign on her counter that read, "Please keep appointments. Help us make medical care affordable for all. Thank you." The receptionist included this message in her reminder calls. Much to everyone's surprise, the no-show rate dropped to less than 5 percent.

These were three tiny, comfortable steps that cost the practice a total of zero dollars. But 10 months later, when the local newspaper published a consumer's survey called "The Best Doctors in Los Angeles," this small, new practice scored *at the top.* The medical practice, which was already financially thriving by this point thanks to word-of-mouth business and the low no-show rate, was now an official blockbuster. And the practice's malpractice claims were the lowest in the area. This good news was mostly due to the doctors' medical skill, but also in part to their habit of making chart notes with the patient present. Because the chart notes were taken immediately, when the doctors' memories were fresh, they tended to be very accurate. And because the chart notes were taken in the patients' presence, the patients felt respected and involved, and therefore less likely to take their complaints to court.

When you apply kaizen to management psychology, you are going to the heart of what TWI and Dr. Deming preached to wartime executives. You are:

- Drawing on your existing resources.
- Inviting your employees to participate.

- Remaining alert for problems to solve.

- Looking for ways to improve service to your customers.

- Making very, very small steps toward change.

Some steps, like the ones taken by the medical practice group, are so small that they can seem ridiculous. But again and again, kaizen works.

善

15

HOW KAIZEN WORKS

To appreciate how kaizen works, you need to know why innovative change often *doesn't* work. Why is radical change so hard? It is because change is uncomfortable. It's more than uncomfortable, actually. It can be terrifying. Over the long course of evolution, our nervous systems have developed an unfortunate feedback loop; our brains are designed to respond to change with fear, but our brains are also designed to respond to fear by shutting down access to the mental resources we need to create change.

To understand this loop, consider the physiology of the brain. To be more accurate, consider your three separate brains. Each of these brains plays a part in regulating your body and mind, but each evolved at a different time.

About 500 million years ago, humans developed their first brain, called the brain stem. This small but vital structure sits atop your spinal cord and sends instructions to your heart, your lungs, and other organs that keep you breathing and functioning.

Just above the brain stem is the midbrain, which is about the size of your fist. This brain came along about 300 million years ago and is called the mammalian brain, because all mammals have one. This is the brain of the emotions, of temperature regulation, and of the survival mechanism.

Surrounding the midbrain is the cerebral cortex, the third and (at a mere 100 million years of age) the most recently developed brain. The cortex is home to the higher functions: thinking, reasoning, and creativity. The cortex is what allows you to make decisions. It lets you analyze your difficulties and imagine solutions. The cortex makes language, inventions, ideas, music, math, science, and art possible. If you want to make changes in your workplace— or anywhere—you need unfettered access to the cortex. Without it, you'll be stuck with the extremely limited, animalistic repertoire of the brain stem and the midbrain.

And there's the rub. When you want to change, it seems only fair that you should put in a request to the cortex and have it get to work on your problem. But instead, the midbrain jumps in and blocks the request. In particular, the amygdala, which you can find at the base of the midbrain, doesn't want the cortex working for you. The amygdala is host to the survival mechanism, the fight-or-flight response that sets off alarm bells whenever it perceives danger. It's designed to keep you safe in times of serious physical peril. It does this by delivering energy to your arms and legs, pumping up your heart, and amping up your stress hormones. It helps you through a crisis by doing one of two things: running away or fighting. Unfortunately, it gets the energy for these activities by stealing them from other sources. Like your digestion. Like your reproductive desire. Like your thinking.

In other words, fear reduces your ability to think creatively and clearly. When you consider the way that the brain evolved, this "problem" makes sense. For hundreds of thousands of years, humans were hunter-gatherers. If you saw a lion charging at you at 40 miles per hour, your brain wanted you to be frightened! And it definitely didn't want the brain's newcomer, the cortex, to stop and ponder the implications of being attacked by the lion. It wanted you to run or pick up a big rock, pronto. So the amygdala shut down the cortex so you could stop thinking and act quickly. It let the cortex mull over the lion much later, when you were safe.

Today, you still need your amygdala to take over in times of real physical danger. The problem is that your amygdala evolved *before* the cortex. The amygdala is not that smart. It can't tell the difference between a charging lion and your shareholders. In fact, it smells danger whenever you try to change your routine—because to the amygdala your routine feels secure, good, and safe. This subconscious mind-body reaction to change is why you may find it so hard to make positive improvements, whether that change is cleaning off your desk or complying with a new reporting system. In the case of the four young doctors, all they wanted to do was find a way to bring in more patients— hardly a threatening life-or-death showdown. Yet they were unable to come up with creative ideas because their alarm systems had closed off access to their best thinking.

You may know a person who reports thinking *more* clearly and experiencing the world *more* vividly when under duress. That's because he or she is able to convert the fear response into something else: excitement. You may have even experienced this on occasion yourself; maybe you once led a charge for major change and relished the task. But most people simply aren't wired to love change, not all the time. For most of us, the mere thought of change makes us frozen or combative. This is not a choice. It's instinct. You can see this effect in employees who respond to change requests by dragging their feet, staring at you blankly, or throwing tantrums. Maybe you've seen it in yourself; maybe you've found it difficult to come up with creative solutions when you're faced with a dire emergency. And that's why innovation, or radical change, rarely works.

Kaizen, however, is different. A kaizen approach asks you to take small steps toward your goal. These steps are so small that they may seem useless, but that's why they work. If the amygdala is like an alarm system, small steps are like cat burglars. Quietly, slowly, and softly, they pad past your fears. Your alarm never goes off. Your body remains relaxed. You retain your access to your rational, creative thoughts.

In the technical, production-oriented applications of kaizen, small steps are seen as a way to produce cumulative change. One tiny change after another tiny change followed by another tiny change, and so on, will eventually deposit you on the doorstep of your goal. This process is summed up in the saying of the ancient Chinese philosopher Lao Tzu: "A journey of a thousand miles begins with the first step."

This kind of accumulating change can be true for management as well. In his business classic *Good to Great*, which analyzes how companies make the shift from ordinary performance into excellence, Jim Collins describes the power of incremental steps:

> We kept thinking we would find the "one big thing," the miracle moment that defined breakthrough. We even pushed for it in our interviews. But . . . no matter how dramatic the end result, the good-to-great transformation never happened in one fell swoop. There was no single defining action, no grand program, no one killer innovation, no solitary lucky break, no wrenching revolution. Good to great comes about by a cumulative process—step by step, action by action, decision by decision, turn by turn of the flywheel—that adds up to sustains and spectacular results.[1]

But from a psychological perspective, kaizen works in other ways, too. You don't always have to take a long series of steps to get where you want to go. In some cases, one or two small steps are all you need, because those steps have a power that's much bigger than their size. This was the case with the receptionist who used a sign and a recorded reminder call to inform patients that no-shows and high medical costs are linked. She took a big problem (the no-show rate) and two small steps later, that problem was solved.

Other times, small steps work in a less direct fashion. In some cases the real power of small steps is that they are creating new neural pathways in your brain. They are literally creating new habits. Before your fears can wake up, a system for change is underway—and it feels familiar, not scary. Eventually, the same actions that would have brought you to your knees earlier now seem safe and easy. This method is especially effective for unblocking your employees' creativity (or yours) and promoting better health habits among your staff. Without fear, and without frustration, very small steps can lead to a revolution.

A kaizen philosophy of small steps will take you to your management goals. In the following pages, I'll show you how small steps can help you:

- Boost morale.

- Contain costs.

- Improve quality.

- Develop new products and services.

- Increase sales.

- Reduce health-care expenses.

In the book's final chapter, I'll give you some suggestions for what to do when even one small step seems too hard.

If you are facing a particular problem, kaizen can help you solve it. But if you let it, kaizen can become more than just a tool. It can become a philosophy that guides your organization to efficiency, service, and creativity. I hope you'll take the journey toward excellence. It begins with one small step.

Chapter Two

Boost Morale

You can improve morale in as little as three minutes a day—by showing appreciation, by defusing difficult people, and by encouraging employees to take small steps toward solving their problems.

Here's a scenario you've seen before: Management realizes that morale is low. Management hires expensive consultants who package a program for improving employee satisfaction. The package includes days for staff picnics and awards ceremonies, free turkeys on Thanksgiving, and summer days spent performing team-building exercises at the beach. Employees who put in heroic "Superman" hours are offered large bonuses. Morale plummets.

What's the reason for morale-building disasters? W. Edwards Deming, the statistician who laid the groundwork for kaizen, felt that it was crucial to pay people fairly for their work. Beyond a reasonable paycheck, however, large rewards and financial incentives tend to fizzle. What people really want, Dr. Deming argued, is to feel appreciated. They want to be heard, to be known, to make a contribution, and to be protected from grossly unfair or unpleasant conditions.

In difficult economic times, when wages are stagnated or low, employees resent the money that's spent on picnics and gifts. They think, "I'd rather have 25 dollars than this turkey." They are also cynical based on the last two or three prepackaged initiatives that have come and gone. Worse, management may be using morale initiatives as a way to avoid supplying the small daily rewards—appreciation, protection, and empowerment—that create a satisfying workplace. Naturally, the best way to create this ideal kaizen environment is one small step at a time.

SMALL GESTURES OF THANKS

I once consulted with a large aerospace firm and was asked to focus on morale problems. Employee surveys reflected widespread dissatisfaction with the management, but the managers couldn't put a finger on the source of the discontent. I began by sitting down with the chief executive officer and asking her for hunches. She listed several reasons employees may have been unhappy, including:

- Recent layoffs.
- Freeze on wage increases.
- Discontinuation of some favorite perks, such as discounts in the cafeteria.

She suspected that the company would have to ride out the unease until the recession ended, hiring could be restarted, and wages and benefits would be back to normal.

Plausible reasoning, but when I interviewed employees at all levels of the organization, the items on the CEO's list seldom came up. Most of the staff understood that the economic climate, not management, was to blame for the company's financial difficulties. Every other corporation in the industry had the same woes. Their actual complaints were much different.

> *"When I walk by the CEO in the hall, she doesn't look me in the eye or greet me."*
>
> *"I've never seen her smile. Maybe things are worse than I thought. What is she not telling us?"*
>
> *"I gave up a weekend with my family to get a report in, and no one thanked me."*
>
> *"I was presenting to the management team, and while I was talking, they were texting."*

Over time, these slights and snubs eroded the staff's belief that they were seen and appreciated. One employee described the accumulating sense of discontent: "No one ever asks us for our ideas," he said. "All we are around here is bad news."

When I shared my findings with the CEO, she was defensive. "I'm not here to hold hands," she said. When I asked her why not, she said, "I don't have time for it! I'm exhausted as it is!" She gestured toward the piles of reports and budget drafts on her desk and to the bank of urgently blinking lights on her office phone.

改

She was right. She didn't have time for a deeply emotional encounter with each employee. Fortunately, a kaizen program for improved employee relations wouldn't take a lot of time, only about three minutes a day. Kaizen made sense for another reason: The CEO was clearly resistant to changing her style of interaction. This was to be expected: remember, resistance to change is natural, because change sets off your brain's alarm system. Very small steps would bypass the alarm response.

I explained that although the steps were small, the dividends, in the form of increased morale and productivity, might be significant. The CEO was reluctant to try a strategy that she felt was outside her job description, but she agreed. She would devote three minutes each day to "hand-holding" activities. These included:

- Greeting employees who passed her in the hall.
- Asking staff about their weekend plans.
- Saying "thank you" when an employee turned in a project.
- Using staff members' names when she knew them.
- Putting away her smartphone during meetings and asking her staff to do the same.

Once she had satisfied her three minutes of employee relations each day, she could go back to her usual ways. (The rule about putting smart phones away was an exception. She and her staff would have to fully commit to that one.) We agreed on a test period of one month.

At the end of the period, the company's human resources department took another survey of employee morale and engagement. Both were up by 60 percent. The CEO's morale was up as well. She reported that when she walked through the building, employees seemed happy to see her; some would stop and ask her questions. She noted, with some surprise, that she enjoyed the interruptions. Rather than see them as a waste of time, she realized that they helped her understand the concerns of the staff more clearly. Her staff meetings, too, had become less formal; contributions flowed more freely. The CEO realized that she'd seen herself as hunkered down inside a fortress, keeping a safe emotional distance from employees who resented her. As she stepped out from behind her protective wall and began making small gestures toward her staff, her understanding shifted. She began to feel that her staff wanted both her and the company to succeed; they were partners, not enemies. She felt more energetic. All this happened without laying out extra money or putting on an employee awards show. It flowed out of three minutes of respect and consideration each day.

When employees praise their bosses for being great communicators, they are not necessarily talking about oratorical skills or hearty, outgoing personalities. Some of the finest leaders are quiet and not given to inspirational speeches. But good leaders take advantage of small moments to connect with the people they encounter at work:

- They make a point of remembering a staff member's name.
- They ask questions and wait for the answers.
- They use the words "thank you" generously.

If you want strong morale, you need to set the emotional tone of your workplace through small moments and small interactions.

THE UNACKNOWLEDGED MORALE-KILLER: DIFFICULT PEOPLE

I am always pleased when I see companies that look beyond the criteria of technical skills when hiring new employees. Successful organizations know that how staff members treat one other, particularity in stressful situations, is essential for high performance and high morale.

I once observed an airline employ an unusual interview process that tested its applicants' willingness to support others. When hiring flight attendants, the airline would put four or five applicants in a circle and ask each to stand up, one at a time, and give a brief speech about why he or she wanted to fly for the company. I was puzzled, because a flight attendant's job requires little public speaking aside from reading announcements over the plane's intercom. When I asked the manager what she was looking for, her answer was impressive: "We don't even listen to the speeches," she said. "We watch the other applicants. Are they keeping eye contact? Do they nod their heads in support or encourage the speaker in any way? We need to know that if there is an unruly passenger at 35,000 feet, a flight attendant will come to a coworker's aid, not look for something to do in the galley."

This manager knew that the best measure of a person's character is to be found in the small gestures—making eye contact or giving an encouraging nod—that suggest a pattern of thoughtful behavior. The same strategy is used by Zappos, the highly successful Internet clothing company. During the interview process for new hires, the Zappos van picks up the applicant at the Las Vegas airport. The applicant tours the offices, meets key employees, is assessed by the HR staff, and is encouraged to wander the facility and talk with any employee he or she wishes. The applicant is then transported back to the airport in the Zappos van. Afterward, the person is vetted by all the interviewers . . . and by the van driver. If the van driver reports that the applicant was inconsiderate, there is no hire.[1] By attending to small moments, these companies are able to winnow out applicants who are likely to bring a "look out for number one" attitude to work, let down their coworkers in a crisis, and destroy morale.

Even with the best of hiring practices, however, you'll find yourself with difficult people in the workplace. They may be your direct reports, or they may be colleagues or supervisors whose behavior affects your staff. You already know the different flavors of difficulty:

- Screamers.

- Passive-aggressive sulkers.
- Slackers.
- Jealous competitors.

改

Some managers try to assist difficult people by sending them to anger-management boot camps or employee-coaching sessions. Sometimes these strategies work and sometimes they don't, but they always eat up resources of time and money. A more common—and even less helpful—"solution" is for management to ignore the problem or pretend that it isn't so bad. Employees may not complain about the situation out loud, but make no mistake: they feel that the boss has left them at the mercy of the difficult person. They perceive, rightly, that their boss is too cowardly or too uninterested in their welfare to intervene. They lose confidence in their manager's ability to run the organization.

MANAGING DIFFICULT PEOPLE: SMALL STEPS TOWARD NEUTRALITY

Often, you can successfully manage a difficult person without forcing a conflict. It starts with you, the manager—and this is true even if the difficult person is not your employee. If your own morale is low from proximity to an irritating supervisor or colleague, your staff will sense your emotional weariness and begin to "catch" it. Eventually, *you* may be seen as a difficult person yourself and the origin of bad feelings that have spread throughout the department.

When handling a difficult person, neutrality is your best tool. Neutrality allows you to behave with dignity instead of moping or exploding. The confidence that you can act maturely and with discernment will improve your own state of mind, and it's reassuring to your staff, who in turn will see that their boss possesses the powers of self-management. Better yet, neutrality is contagious. Difficult people are usually difficult because they are afraid and upset. When you are calmer, they are calmer. When they are calmer, they are less defensive and will give you more of an opportunity to work through a problem.

Although it's easy to see the benefit of neutrality, achieving it is more challenging. Fortunately, you can reprogram your response to a difficult person.

When you have five minutes, try these short steps:

1. Begin by thinking of the difficult person and identifying the specific behaviors you dislike. Common complaints include aggressive coworkers who dismiss your ideas or employees who interrupt you and seldom seem to listen.

2. What is your explanation for these annoying behaviors? Some common responses include:

   a. *"He wouldn't treat me this way if I were a man (or woman)."*

   b. *"She is bullying me because she thinks I am weak."*

   c. *"She thinks she knows more than me and is trying to prove it."*

   d. *"He likes to take advantage of people."*

   e. *"He thinks I am stupid or lazy."*

3. Apply what I call the "brain tumor test." Imagine that you were shown a magnetic resonance imaging (MRI) of the difficult person's brain and learned that a benign but inoperable brain tumor, pressing on his or her frontal lobes, is the reason for the annoying behaviors you listed. How would that change your emotional response to those behaviors? If you are like most people, you'd feel less hurt or angry. You'd take the actions less personally. That's because the real source of your upset is not the bad behavior itself. The real source of your irritation is the explanation you are giving yourself for the behavior.

Thinking of the person as suffering from a brain tumor may reduce your distress—until you return to reality. In fact, the person probably doesn't have a brain tumor. So substitute a much more likely explanation: This person behaves poorly because he or she is afraid. The behavior has nothing to do with you. There is much fear in the workplace but very little opportunity to recognize or express it. People who are afraid of being inadequate, dismissed, or not liked often respond with anger, condescension, or competitive behavior. When you can see that fear causes difficult behavior, it's easier not to take it personally. Just as if a brain tumor was the cause.

Assuming that fear is the motivator for difficult behavior may seem like an overly simple way to address a complicated, festering problem, but it works. It also sets the stage for taking two more kaizen steps toward neutrality.

MANAGING DIFFICULT PEOPLE: TWO MORE STEPS

I recently had an opportunity to describe these two kaizen steps to a valuable midlevel manager whose department was performing poorly. Upper management asked me to consult with him and investigate. It turned out that the manager, Bill, was willing to talk candidly. He acknowledged that he'd been struggling lately. He also confided in me that the reason for his problems was *his* new supervisor, Charlene. Bill perceived Charlene as inconsistent, less than truthful, demeaning to his direct reports, and more interested in looking good and making her next promotion than building a high-functioning team.

Charlene often interacted with Bill's staff. He knew that her attitude was having a poisonous effect on them, but he wasn't sure how to approach Charlene about the matter. He knew that she often reacted defensively. Bill imagined a scenario in which Charlene was angry with him for bringing up the problem and he in turn became furious with her for being so difficult. He disliked the thought of behaving unprofessionally; he wondered if starting a fight with his boss would lead to her firing him. Bill brooded over his situation. Unable to address his negative thoughts about Charlene, they took on a larger and larger presence in his mind. In the meantime, Bill's department continued to suffer.

I sympathized with Bill. Most of us know what it's like to be held hostage to an explosive personality. I agreed with Bill that he should not confront Charlene until he could feel less provoked by her behavior. Yet Charlene's actions were, in fact, provocative. How could he change feelings that felt so logical, so justifiable?

Bill's first goal was to remain neutral in Charlene's presence. We went through the steps I outlined above, including the brain tumor test. "Yes," Bill acknowledged, "I can see that she might be acting this way out of fear. Don't ask me what those fears might be, though." For our purposes, it didn't matter. What mattered is that her problematic attitude probably didn't flow out of a personal disdain for him. It was all about *her*—her doubts and her fears about her own performance.

However, this new way of thinking wasn't enough to dissolve Bill's emotional reaction to Charlene. He was still consumed by his angry thoughts about her. We had to find a way to change his behavior without setting off a serious stress response that would sabotage his efforts.

I reassured Bill that he shouldn't expect to make huge progress in his attitude right away. Incremental changes were enough. I also suggested that he take two additional small steps toward a more neutral position:

1. Ask Charlene a series of questions.

2. Offer Charlene a series of compliments.

Both steps were designed to help Bill feel less oppressed and more professional. *Asking questions*, the first small step, is an antidote to stress. Another person's challenging behavior can activate your amygdala—the brain's alarm center—and flood your brain with anger and worry. The creative cortex is compromised or completely shut down. But curiosity pulls you away from the stress response and allows you to access your cortex, the thinking brain. Curiosity doesn't judge or panic. Curiosity says: "Well, that's interesting."

Compliments, the second small step, are a more advanced form of neutrality. They are designed to help you counter your painful awareness of another person's weaknesses and allow you to see him or her as a flawed but rounded person.

善

33

Bill accepted my suggestions and explanation, but only in theory. He was still consumed by his angry thoughts about Charlene. He couldn't pay her a compliment, he said, without feeling like a hypocrite. The thought made his head hurt.

I suggested that Bill proceed anyway, but very slowly. I asked him to forget about the compliments for the moment; right now, all he had to do was ask her one open-ended question a day. He wasn't supposed to persuade, cajole, or demonstrate his superiority to Charlene. Instead, he was to ask questions that implied no judgment or opinion. He could try asking questions that began "What are your thoughts about . . . ?" or "Can you tell me more about . . . ?"

Some of Bill's questions included:

> *"What did you think of the budget meeting today?"*

> *"I noticed you biked to work this morning. What do you enjoy most about cycling? How do you handle the traffic?"*

> *"Was I reading you right at the planning session? You seemed to have some additional ideas to talk about."*

After two weeks, Bill reported that he was slightly less reactive with Charlene. He was ready to try the next step: compliments.

The thought of complimenting Charlene made Bill upset. "I'd feel like a fake," he said. The kaizen mentality never asks us to take a step that feels too big or too intimidating. But it also asks us not to give up. Instead, I asked Bill to make the step smaller. I suggested he begin by simply thinking of one kind thought about Charlene each day and e-mailing it to me. His first message to me read: "*I feel silly doing this but . . . Charlene was gracious to a housekeeper today.*" His messages soon became more detailed:

> "*Charlene has skills in running a meeting; she asked for input on the cost overruns and seemed to listen carefully.*"

> "*Charlene knows the business, and sometimes she has a perspective I hadn't thought of.*"

> "*She fired someone who should have been let go a long time ago. She can be decisive.*"

Bill continued these daily e-mails for two weeks, long enough to change his habitual style of interaction. (Sometimes you need even longer periods of time to break a consistently negative pattern. That's fine. Kaizen asks you not to hurry.) I asked Bill if he was ready for the next step: either giving Charlene a compliment directly or, if that was too hard, saying something positive about her to another person. The benefits would be twofold. He would feel more detached from his anger, and the accumulating compliments might have a softening effect on the fears that drove Charlene's bad behavior, at least a little.

Bill wisely chose to compliment Charlene to others first. When he was in the elevator with Charlene's supervisor, he commented how knowledgeable Charlene was. He told a colleague he appreciated that Charlene made her expectations clear (leaving out his opinions about those expectations). Then Bill directly complimented Charlene on her expertise whenever he consulted with her about technical issues. After two more weeks of daily compliments to Charlene, either directly or to others, Bill felt confident in his neutral stance toward her. Although her behavior hadn't changed, Bill felt he was ready to share one—just one—of his concerns about her working style with her.

During the interview, Bill was not perfectly comfortable, but he was more nervous than he was angry. This was a good sign: nervousness is closer to a neutral stance than anger is. He was calm enough to recall that a decade of research has shown that it's better not to confront someone with a negatively toned question, such as "Why don't you want to play as a team?" or "Why can't you be straightforward with me?" Such questions only invite the other person's brain to rehearse and strengthen excuses for the poor behavior.

Bill had the presence of mind to take a different approach. He asked Charlene, "Are you aware of your communication style in meetings? Can I give you some feedback?"

Much to his surprise and my relief, Charlene acknowledged feeling overwhelmed by the new position and stumbling a bit. I thought it was also quite possible that

改善

The Art of Compliments

Managers are sometimes taught to use the "sandwich technique" of giving a compliment, sliding in a criticism, and then giving another compliment. This is a small step with good intentions, but unfortunately, employees soon pick up on the technique. They start to dismiss the initial compliment, assuming it is merely a setup for the unpleasant criticism that is to come. A history of appreciation prior to offering criticism is more effective; the person feels more trusting toward you and less entrenched in his or her position.

When you need to confront someone about his or her behavior, spend a few weeks seeding the relationship with small compliments. You don't need to resort to insincere praise. One form of complimenting is to notice the person's efforts. ("I saw you worked at your desk through lunch. Thanks.") Another kind of compliment recognizes the other person's individuality. It takes the subtle form of remembering employees' names, knowing the names of their spouses and children, and asking about their weekend or vacation.

Charlene picked up on his change of tone and was disarmed by his jitters. Soon after, Bill's department returned to its previous level of productivity—likely a result of Charlene's improved skills *and* Bill's less distracted, less aggrieved style.

As Bill continues his management career, it will be his task to notice small gestures and revealing statements when he is hiring team members and to solve small personnel problems before they balloon into disasters. When problems do arise, he can draw on his own experience to counsel staff members to take small steps toward productive neutrality—and he can explain that there is no better training ground for keeping your cool than working with a really abrasive person. As the Zen proverb says, "Blessed are your enemies, for they allow you to grow."

ALLOW EMPLOYEES TO IMPROVE THEIR CONDITIONS

We all have the inner drive to learn, to contribute, and to solve problems. Too often management puts the brakes on this impulse. When you are feeling pressured, it's tempting to reply to an employee's idea or suggestion with one of these responses:

> *"We've already tried that."*
>
> *"That won't work."*
>
> *"Let management worry about that."*
>
> *"That's not the way it's done."*

Yet staff can easily become cynical if their suggestions for improvement are not handled skillfully and promptly. Once, while I was preparing for a lecture at a high-end hotel in Los Angeles, a staff member walked by me in tears. When I asked her why she was upset, she explained that she'd made a suggestion at a managers' meeting earlier that day. An hour after the meeting, she was called into the general managers' office and reprimanded for "not being a team player." If the hotel's upper management continues to push away suggestions, employees will echo the complaint made in the aerospace company: "All we are around here is bad news." As Robert (Bob) Herres, former CEO of USAA, said, "If employees feel like they are throwing pennies down a bottomless well and they never hear a splash, they are going to stop throwing pennies."[2] But a receptive and respectful management can unleash the creative energies of an organization.

I am reminded of an orthopedic surgeon whose receptionist was low-spirited and sullen. After attending one of my lectures, he returned to his office and asked the receptionist to pinpoint what irritated her most about her job—and challenged her to think of the smallest change possible that would address the problem. As it turned out, the woman felt frustrated because the doctor often ran late. Patients would rush to get to the office on time, only to sit 45 minutes or so in the waiting area. The receptionist hated having to manage a waiting room full of grumpy clients. Although she had complained to the doctor about the scheduling problem, he'd always explained that he couldn't predict which patients would need extra time (a constant difficulty in medical scheduling).

The situation turned when the surgeon, in an encouraging tone, suggested that the receptionist could change the process on *her* end of things. "What's a small step you could take that would improve the problem?" he asked her. When she realized her supervisor was open to ideas, she produced one: Since most patients carry cell phones, she would call them as soon as she was aware the doctor was running late and advised them of their new appointment time. It worked. This was one of those small steps that had a large effect. The patients were grateful. Instead of berating her for the doctor's lateness, the patients now walked into the office and thanked the receptionist for her consideration. The doctor applied this kaizen technique to the entire team, asking his staff to think of a small thing that irritated them and a small step to improve it. At the end of the year, he tallied up the small improvements the staff had made. The total was more than 200 improvements.

Expect stumbles. (Stumbles are small steps, too.) The kaizen process can easily be disrupted by poor responses to suggestions. It is crucial that you respond to suggestions—or criticisms—promptly and attentively. No doubt that if you ask employees to solve their problems, you'll receive some unworkable suggestions. A staff member might suggest cutting out a service that is critical to the organization's functioning or might want to cut corners in a way that jeopardizes safety.

I once asked a Toyota manager what the managers do when they receive poor suggestions. He responded, "These are very important to us because they tell us our training of this employee has been ineffective and we can now help this person to improve."

改

Be careful not to dismiss a suggestion before considering it carefully. A beautiful feature of kaizen is that when suggestions are truly small ones, there is often little risk involved. You can give your employees latitude to pilot their own ideas, fail, and come up with something new. As they realize that you are committed to nurturing their powers of discovery and imagination, energy and creativity will increase. Kaizen creates a virtuous cycle.

Kaizen Pathway: Morale in Minutes

改善

Low morale is one of those global problems in a company. It's hard to pinpoint exactly who suffers from it and who doesn't, and it's often impossible to know where it began. For that reason, it seems to most managers as if the solution to low morale should be global, too—with a high cost, high effort, and a high degree of complication.

But you can strengthen morale in just a few minutes each day. This chapter suggests a few ways to do it, but the very best kaizen steps are often the ones you create yourself. To come up with a kaizen plan to boosting your staff's attitude, ask yourself these questions:

1. "What is one small thing I can do to increase morale that will take no more than five minutes each day?"
2. "What is one small thing I can do to increase morale that will take no more than three minutes each day?"
3. "What is one small thing I can do to increase morale that will take only one minute each day?"

41

Write out these questions and put them in a place where you can easily see them. Don't worry at first about coming up with answers; just read the questions to yourself at least once every day. Soon enough, you'll surprise yourself with creative responses. Choose one or two responses that seem so easy that you know you cannot fail. If they seem absurdly small or unlikely to work, that's even better. Remember, one way kaizen works is by tricking your inner alarm system into thinking that there is absolutely no danger of change.

Chapter Three

CUT COSTS

A kaizen approach to cost control is a state of mind, one that engages employees to constantly pare away any process that does not contribute to quality or service.

Kaizen is a small but powerful tool for controlling and reducing costs. Unlike other approaches to cutting expenses, kaizen does not compromise the quality of the product or service. Kaizen does not undercut the well-being of employees. It does not cover up for corporate inefficiency by raising costs to the consumer. Kaizen is not a one-time maneuver made out of desperation.

In kaizen organizations, every employee is expected to remain constantly alert for wasted resources. When employees find a process that does not increase the value or quality of the experience, the company trims it away. This formula for cost control is efficient and effective, thanks to the clearheadedness of its basic assumption: *the people who are best able to reduce the costs of the job are the people who are actually performing that job.*

Yet it's not applied very often. Why not?

I'm reminded of an interview with Colleen Barrett, a past CEO of Southwest Airlines. Barrett explained that people often ask her the secret of Southwest Airlines' success. "We tell them," she said, "that it's how we treat our people. And they say, 'No, really, what is it?'"[1]

Elegantly simple concepts are often discarded *because* they are elegantly simple concepts. We mistake simplicity for stupidity. It may seem futile to depend on employees for cost control, but if you invite them to take small steps toward saving money, they will. Although small savings cannot always rescue a company from an entrenched philosophy of bloat and waste—if you have been heedless of overspending for years, big cuts may be unavoidable—they can pull you through a particular crisis, such as an increase in the price of fuel or an economic slump. Better still, a kaizen approach to cost control can help you avoid major budget problems in the first place, and it will give your company a reputation for great value.

However, don't just put the responsibility for lowering costs onto your employee's shoulders and walk away. This big step will create the kind of fear that blocks change. Instead, shape your employees' approach to their daily tasks so that they can spot opportunities for savings. Expect their full engagement. Help them bypass their fear of mak-

改

ing suggestions that are wrong or silly. Help them bypass their fear of *you*. This chapter will show you how.

THINK OUTSIDE THE SUGGESTION BOX

Have you ever lifted the lid on an employee suggestion box? This corporate tool supposedly encourages employees to spot waste or suggest ways to streamline the manufacturing process. Often there is a financial reward for suggestions that lead to significant savings. But according to Alan G. Robinson and Sam Stern in *Corporate Creativity: How Innovation and Improvement Actually Happen*, the average American employee makes only one suggestion every six years. What you'll really find inside the box are a couple of greasy sandwich wrappers (especially if the box is in the break room) and a few uninspired "suggestions" that are really complaints in disguise:

> *"We need more vacation time."*
>
> *"Fire everyone in upper management."*
>
> *"Get better equipment. My back hurts."*

If you want to unlock your employees' natural desire to contribute and feel engaged at work, you should start by taking down the suggestion box. Managers who post suggestion boxes usually have good intentions, but they are making several missteps that block their workers' creativity and energy. By relying on the suggestion box—especially when there is an associated system of financial rewards—

managers unwittingly stifle creativity, promote an atmo-sphere of secrecy, and suggest that no one is really paying attention anyway. The good news is that there are very small steps you can take to cultivate and harvest your staff's natural creativity.

COST CONTROL STEP 1:
OFFER SMALL REWARDS OR NONE AT ALL

Although employee suggestion plans in the United States tend to flatline, in Japan they are wildly, consistently suc-cessful: the average Japanese worker proposes 18 ideas every year. That's one every three weeks. The suggestions are also smart. In Japan, nearly 90 percent of employee suggestions are adopted, compared to 38 percent of those in the United States.

What accounts for this difference? In the United States, employees are commonly offered cash rewards in proportion to the amount of money the suggestion saves the company. The idea is that employees will be motivated to save big money, because they'll receive big money in return. In Japan, the cash rewards are very modest . . . or there are *no cash rewards at all*.

Counterintuitive? Yes. But years of psychological stud-ies into human motivation are illuminating. There are two basic types of motivation: intrinsic and extrinsic. "Extrinsic motives" can be found outside of one's self: these are driv-ers such as money and impressive titles. "Intrinsic motives" come from inside. These are the desire to contribute, to take pride in one's work, and to be engaged in a meaning-ful task. As I've noted earlier, Dr. Edwards Deming argued that it is important to attend to extrinsic motivation by paying workers a good wage. (He would also advise against an overwhelming discrepancy in pay between executives and line workers.) But large performance incentives dis-rupt intrinsic motivation. People have an inner drive to do meaningful work; they want to be challenged and proud of what they do. This universal desire to feel engaged is the birth mother of kaizen. And although extrinsic motiva-tion works fine for rote tasks—it does help to pay people more to stick with tedious work—for creative or thought-ful endeavors it is destructive. In 2009, a team at the Lon-don School of Economics reviewed more than 50 studies of financial incentives and concluded that they result in a "negative impact on overall performance."[2] When people feel that a cash reward is their only reason to work hard, their minds go to sleep.

If you have an incentive-based suggestion program, consider the messages it might unintentionally convey:

> *"You employees are lazy, indifferent people who have to be bribed into making contributions to the organization."*

> *"If you have a good idea, you'd better protect it from other workers who might steal it and claim the reward."*

> *"I'm not interested in a suggestion unless it leads to an instant jackpot for the company."*

> *"Smaller suggestions aren't worth making."*

Offering large bonuses is a swift, sure method of squelching your employees' innate desire for engagement. But it's not wise to give up rewards altogether. The twentieth-century psychologist B. F. Skinner proved beyond doubt that an intelligent system of rewards, known as "positive reinforcement," can mold human behavior. This is the psychological knowledge that allows us to train dolphins to perform flips by giving them toys or attention and to teach children to clean their rooms with the reward of silver stars stuck to a chart.

改

48

The key is to make the rewards small. When Japanese workers make useful suggestions, they receive an award, but that award has an average value of about 4 dollars. The near-worthlessness of the reward is the key to its success. Small rewards speak directly to the employee's internal motivation. Small rewards say, "Management sees that you have a desire to improve and contribute, and we appreciate it."

A remarkable example of a successful small reward comes from Continental Airlines. In this case, Continental Airlines was seeking to reduce wasted time (which is often wasted money). When Gordon M. Bethune became Continental's CEO, the company was ranked a dismal seventh among airlines for on-time performance. Bethune announced that every one of Continental Airlines' 30 thousand employees would receive a 65-dollar bonus if and when the airline scored in the top four airlines for performance times. People quickly started to work together, looking for ways they could do better—as opposed to looking for whom to blame. Between January 1995 and March 1995, Continental Airlines took its on-time arrival status from seventh to first. Sixty-five dollars was not a huge sum of money to most of its workers, especially the pilots and flight schedulers. But as is often the case, the relatively small reward worked to focus and motivate the working group.[3]

Other examples of successful small rewards include:

- Sending a personal note from management to the employee.
- Finding out how the employee takes his or her morning coffee and coming by with a cup.
- Visiting with the employee personally during the day.
- Sitting down to talk over an employee's suggestion, asking how he or she came up with the idea, and offering your thanks.

If these rewards seem shoddy, bear this in mind: The most commonly cited reason that people leave a job is because they feel underappreciated. If you reward cost-saving ideas with your time and interest, suggestions will flow in.

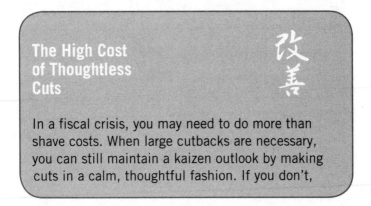

The High Cost of Thoughtless Cuts

In a fiscal crisis, you may need to do more than shave costs. When large cutbacks are necessary, you can still maintain a kaizen outlook by making cuts in a calm, thoughtful fashion. If you don't,

49

you're at risk for what your grandparents might have called a "false economy," which is a move that ends up costing more than it saves.

The fate of Circuit City, the electronics retail chain, is a case study in the perils of thinking carelessly, at least when it comes to reducing costs. In 2001, Jim Collins listed Circuit City in his classic book *Good to Great* as an outstanding success story marked by extraordinary stock performance. But in 2007 the CEO decided to save money by firing the experienced floor staff, who earned more. The company kept on only the newer, less expensive—and less knowledgeable—employees. Circuit City is now gone, defunct. The company cut costs by cutting its reputation for service and handed its customers a compelling reason to shop elsewhere.

Or think of Toyota, which cut costs by scrimping on the quality of its parts. A series of high-profile recalls tarnished this once-sterling brand and made drivers wary.

Or look at what happened to a county board of supervisors in my home state of Washington. Under severe budget pressure, the board decided to cut costs by reducing services to the mentally ill. The patients lost their counseling and their medications. Unfortunately, these patients did not disappear when their treatment ended. They became increasingly unstable, agitated, and reliant on illegal substances. Their behavior landed many of them in the county jail—which is required by law to provide medical treatment, including counseling and psychiatric drugs. Faced with an onslaught of patient-prisoners, the jail paid much higher prices for the drugs than the mental health department had. Why? Because the mental health department had long ago negotiated with the pharmaceutical companies for steep discounts. The jail had not done so, having had no reason to. The county paid more, not less, for mental health services that year. The county's need to cut costs was real, but its method of saving money was an illusion.

善

51

COST CONTROL STEP 2:
ASK SMALL QUESTIONS

I've known managers who look to their employees for continual improvement but are too aggressive in their tactics. Imagine a supervisor who summons everyone to a meeting and barks, "How much money are *you* going to save this company today?" He wants to instill a sense of urgency in his staff and appeal to their heroic impulses. If they know he expects them to move mountains, he reasons, they will figure out a way do it.

Unfortunately, no mountains are moved using this approach. The employees feel uncomfortable and embarrassed. Some of them give vague answers that are designed to get their boss to calm down and leave them alone to do their jobs. Their boss's question is *too* big.

Questions such as "How can you save the company millions of dollars?" or "What's a way to revolutionize our production process?" set off the brain's alarm system and have a paralyzing effect. They are just questions, but our amygdala think we are in a major crisis. Blood flows toward our limbs—we get ready to kick and punch, ready to run—and away from the cerebral cortex, where it's most needed. In response to a big question, most of us will mentally run away—*hey, it's not my job to figure that one out*—or stall out with a noise that we can imagine sounds something like *uhhhhhhhh* or *pfffffft*.

For greater success, try a softer approach:

> *"Can you think of one way you could shave a few dollars off our expenses?"*

> *"Is there a small step we could take to reduce waste?"*

> *"What is the very smallest thing we could do to save money?"*

Or try an employee favorite, which is to encourage your staff to think about their sources of irritation at work. People are frustrated when they are doing something that seems meaningless or wasteful, or that makes them look bad in front of customers. All are possibilities for kaizen change.

This strategy works because it's less intimidating. A small question is so unthreatening that it quietly creeps past the brain's alarm system. A small question makes it safe for creative impulses to come out and play. You might not get an answer to your small question right away, but keep asking. Ask every day, or at every staff meeting. Take down the suggestion box and replace it with a sign asking your question.

The brain's principal criterion for deciding what to store and what to discard is this: *repetition*. Ask *any* question often enough, and the brain will have no option but to store it—and to mull it over. Soon enough, your staff will find themselves viewing their task in a new way. They'll look for wasted actions and wasted resources.

Like the designers at Dell Computer, your staff will look for ways to eliminate even a single screw from a product, as long as change does not lower the quality of the product. (At Dell, one less screw means a savings of roughly four seconds per machine built.)[4] Or your staff will place an order for paper and wonder whether there is a better, cheaper supplier. Cost savings will become an intriguing game. Employees will enjoy themselves more.

Small questions should be a part of your company's day in, day out cost-saving routine, but you can use them in dire circumstances, too. If your company is in financial crisis, these small questions will have an effect that is surprisingly soothing. In a time of distress, the brain craves action. Small questions allow the brain to get to work and start solving problems.

COST-CUTTING STEP 3:
CONNECT THE SAVINGS TO YOUR CORPORATE MISSION

A suggestion box on a wall, or an electronic bulletin board with no obvious readers, is disconnected from the company. The implied message is that suggestions are separate

改

善

改

54

Small Questions, Small Suggestions

A predictable advantage of small questions is that they lead to suggestions for small improvements. You should treasure small suggestions. Whereas large suggestions tend to alter the company's mission ("Instead of selling baked goods, let's sell men's sportswear!"), small ideas are likely to save you money without radically disturbing the company's culture or its systems.

Sometimes little changes gather an accumulating force. A former CEO of McDonald's, Jack M. Greenberg, pointed out that every six seconds saved at the drive-through window increased sales by 1 percent.[5]

When American Airlines needed to offset a nine-figure increase in fuel costs, it did so through a series of small steps:

- Flight attendants asked passengers to lower their shades before disembarking (to keep the plane cooler).
- Unused ovens were jettisoned.
- Pilots plugged into ground power when waiting at the gate, instead of drawing on the plane's auxiliary power.

> The pilot who initiated the savings program later remarked, "What I learned is we could save $100 million, $25 at a time."[6] An ongoing benefit is that each successful small suggestion influences the mindset of employees, who will now feel inspired to look for further ways to cut expenses.
>
> One small idea sometimes leads *directly* to substantial savings, all on its own. After medical personnel in the intensive-care units of Michigan hospitals began to follow a simple five-step checklist when inserting catheters, the rate of catheter infections dropped from 4 percent to zero. The steps saved an estimated 1,500 lives and more than $200 million.[7] Never let "common sense" dictate that big problems always demand big solutions.

from the employees' real work. It's something they can do on the side.

You'll have more success with kaizen cost control if you integrate it into your corporate mission. This was the source of Toyota's success in its heyday; it steeped employees in the culture of kaizen, teaching them that every task held the potential to be more effective and more efficient.

David Welch in a *BusinessWeek* article tells the story of an assembly-line worker at a Toyota plant in Kentucky. The worker was reaching for a bolt in a bin when his kaizen consciousness led him to ask the foreman, "How much does Toyota pay for this bin?" The worker had seen one at a box store in town and wanted to compare the prices. The foreman did not know but promised to investigate. The cost of the bin at the local store was a fraction of what Toyota was paying; the savings to the company were substantial. The employee was not under specific orders to cut costs. He considered it his job to improve the process wherever he could. The foreman, too, contributed to the improvement, because he was receptive to questions.[8]

改

United Parcel Service (UPS) is another company with a kaizenlike attention to detail. (The company saves space at its dispatch centers by mandating that its brown vans park exactly five inches apart, with the rearview mirrors overlapping.) Using kaizen thinking, the UPS engineers recognized that left-hand turns are costly to the company; trucks have to idle longer at intersections, consuming extra fuel and taking up precious time. The engineers edited their GPS software to reduce left-hand turns. UPS has estimated that in one year, this change saved 28.5 million miles off their usual routes and saved 3 million gallons of gas. And within five months of the change, carbon dioxide emissions were reduced by more than a thousand metric tons in New York City alone.[9]

You can also get employees on board a specific cost-cutting project. The state of Arizona, in deep budgetary trouble, issued a plea to all its employees: *"We need everyone to save money so that we in turn can save your jobs."* With that request in mind, a state highway patrol officer was looking for a way to spend his downtime while waiting for speeders to rush by. He decided to read the car's owner's manual and discovered that the state was changing the oil more often than was recommended by the manufacturer.

He sent his idea up the chain of command, and the resulting savings totaled more than $100 thousand.[10]

Warning: Use Small Acts for Good

改善

Successful managers recognize the vital role of their small acts in defining and sustaining a cost-cutting project. Less successful leaders allow small, thoughtless actions to undercut their mission.

I once worked with a teaching hospital that was facing financial challenges. The CEO took the unusual step of attending the meetings of various staffs: physicians, nurses, tech workers, and custodians. He implored each employee to find ways to reduce costs. People rallied to the cause, and suggestions streamed in.

The CEO, of course, was also looking for ways to reduce costs, and he decided to end the practice of giving free cafeteria lunches to the physicians. Everyone was disappointed but could not fault his reasoning. But then the CEO was observed going through the cafeteria line himself . . . without paying. It took only a few minutes for word of this leadership mistake to spread throughout the hospital. Suggestions for cost cutting virtually stopped. Small acts have powerful, symbolic meanings to staff.

Airlines, whose fixed costs are very high, often taken a kaizen approach to savings. Herb Kelleher, the former CEO of Southwest Airlines, wrote a letter asking each of the company's employees to save $5 a day. One flight attendant suggested using plain, unmarked trash bags instead of paying for the bags marked with the airline's logo. The small idea resulted in an annual savings of $300 thousand. Another employee took the stairs instead of the elevator to save electricity. At the end of the year, the company cut costs by more than 5 percent.[11]

改

COST-CUTTING STEP 4:
BE RECEPTIVE TO SUGGESTIONS

Employees are afraid of looking foolish. They are also afraid of making you angry. They won't feel safe telling you their cost-saving suggestions unless you actively insist on their input. When you adopt kaizen, you give your employees an assignment to look for cost cuts, but you are still in charge. You need to convey authority, and you are responsible for filtering and evaluating the ideas.

You must also be confident enough to say to your staff, "Our system reflects the best ideas we've had so far. But I expect you to tell me if you see a way to do things better." When do you say this? That depends on your personal style. You can send this message:

- To each new hire when he or she begins work at your company.

- At the opening of every day in an internal e-mail.

- With all of your internal e-mail correspondences, as part of your signature line.

The fastest way to kill kaizen is to ask for suggestions and then let them languish on your desk. Setting up a procedure for managing suggestions is crucial. If your organization or department is small enough, provide a way for employees to contribute their suggestions personally, by talking face-to-face to you or to another manager. This allows you to thank the employee immediately and either provide instant feedback or make a promise to think through the idea and follow it up.

Large corporations can make use of alternate systems. Bruce Power, a Canadian nuclear power company, maintains kiosks throughout its facility where suggestions can be submitted. The accounting firm PricewaterhouseCoopers, with employees all over the world, directs staff to send suggestions to a company website. More than 60 percent of the staff has participated.

These systems aren't really all that different from a suggestion box—with the important exception, each suggestion is carefully considered and the employees know it. Thanks to management's attention, these systems don't give off that black-hole-of-meaninglessness quality you feel when you see a suggestion box.

If you must use a less personal system, be sure that employees know who will read their suggestions and when they will hear back about them. As you sift through suggestions, take each one seriously. Remember not to confuse simplicity with stupidity; questions that appear to be naïve may hold the seeds of genius. If the suggestion works, put it in place. Thank the employee, bestow whatever small reward is appropriate, and encourage him or her to send more ideas your way. When the suggestion betrays ignorance, you should *also* thank the employee—and then take the opportunity to retrain the employee. As always, kaizen offers opportunities to learn.

改

60

Kaizen Pathway: Small Questions

改善

The small question, *"What is one way you can save the company 1 dollar today?"* is an effective way to reduce wasted resources. If you ask the question often enough, your employees will begin—almost automatically—to seek small cost savings. So will you.

But the power of small questions goes beyond cutting costs. Small questions can help you spot new ways to continually make your department better. Here are a few small questions, designed to elicit the best from you and your department. Remember, answers may not come to you right away. But if you ask a question regularly and wait patiently for an answer, you will be rewarded.

For general excellence, ask:

"What is one small way I could improve the customer experience?"

"What is one small irritation I can try to address?"

To mine a relationship for its insights, ask:

"Is there a person whose opinion I haven't heard in a while? Can I ask that person for some small feedback?"

To see yourself and others with less pessimism and greater clarity, ask:

"Is there a person here who drives me crazy? What is one small thing that is good about this person?"

"What is one small thing that is good or strong about me?"

善

61

Chapter Four

IMPROVE QUALITY

Improve your ability to spot little mistakes. Small oversights, glitches, and snags may seem merely annoying at first, but they can develop into quality-control calamities if you don't address them early on.

Some of you are old enough to remember a time when it was routine to take a new car back to the dealer a dozen times in its first year. The more you drove the car, the more defects you found. You'd go out one morning in the early fall and discover that your engine didn't like cool weather. You'd reach to switch on an interior light . . . and the toggle would fall out. The passenger seat might start to wobble. If the dashboard clock told the correct time, you considered yourself lucky.

These manufacturing mistakes slipped through, time and time again, even though the automotive industry tried hard to avoid them. The industry's foundational production technique, the assembly line, was supposed to produce car components that were consistent and that were precisely attached. For decades, workers on the line built the cars and quality control staff stood at the line's end, inspecting the cars and looking for defects that required correction. Yet defects kept slipping through, and customers kept complaining.

Enter kaizen. When Toyota began to rebuild its auto factories after World War II, the level of wartime devastation meant that the company was starting from scratch, giving its leaders an opportunity to think about the production process differently. One of Toyota's executives, Taiichi Ohno, visited auto factories in Detroit several times to learn from the competition. There, Ohno found the assembly lines and "rework areas" filled with broken pieces and leftover parts. Ohno had learned about kaizen from W. Edwards Deming; the sight of waste—antithetical to kaizen and certainly not a luxury his company could afford—bothered him.

Ohno went back to Toyota City in Japan and introduced a revolutionary change. At each step of the assembly line, he placed a rope called the andon cord. Ohno instructed the line workers that if they saw an error they should pull the cord, which would slow or stop the line so that engineers, line workers, and even suppliers could confer and correct the mistake. If a worker was putting on a front tire and saw scratches on the fender, he'd pull the andon cord. If he noticed that an assembly on the door handle didn't fit correctly, he'd pull the andon cord.

Ohno's move defied the logic of the time. His competitors thought he was crazy. How could you manufacture thousands of cars each day if you were stopping the line to fix what were often minor defects? Yet paying attention to little problems turned out to be the most efficient way to build cars. Attend to a scratched fender on the line, and you do more than fix one scratch. You head off bigger problems because you learn that the scratch is an early warning sign that a piece of equipment is malfunctioning; now you can repair the equipment while it is still relatively easy to repair. You avoid a complete breakdown, and higher repair expenses, later on. Even better, your customers aren't coming in with complaints about their fenders. Soon Toyota developed a reputation for quality that drew millions of people to their products.

Kaizen requires that we look for, and address, mistakes while they are still small. That sounds easy to accomplish, but in fact it's tempting to overlook or misread seemingly trifling problems until they expand into catastrophes. Here's a cautionary tale from another industry: well before the final, fatal flight of the space shuttle *Challenger*, NASA engineers noticed some scorching on the shuttle's O-rings. Although the O-rings are crucial—they prevent fuel from burning through the shuttle's rocket boosters—this "small" glitch was ignored. As the shuttle had survived the scorching, NASA reasoned that the scorching must not be an important problem. And with each flight that passed in which the O-rings were scorched, the more logical it seemed to redefine the burn marks as a normal aspect of operations—until the morning of January 28, 1986, when one of the O-rings burned completely through during liftoff. The shuttle exploded, and all seven astronauts on board died.

You don't have to look to major disasters to see the wisdom of noticing and exploring small mistakes. Perhaps you can recall an employee whom you were forced to fire or a creative project that ended painfully. Were there not small signs, little indications along the way, that things weren't going in the direction you had hoped? It's human nature to overlook the small concerns when you are under pressure to achieve a goal, to meet a sales target, or to fill the position. But as these small problems grow larger and larger, it becomes even more difficult to tame them. Eventually they create such chaos that you are left with undesirable but unavoidable lines of actions: halt production, clean up the mess, haul off the waste, or call in the lawyers. Unless you are committed to addressing small mistakes, you risk having your attention hijacked by very big problems.

BE TRANSPARENT, NOT PERFECT

IndyCar racing is a fast, dangerous sport. With open cockpits that leave their heads exposed and open wheels that are unprotected by fenders, drivers send their cars around the track at 200 miles per hour or more—and they maintain those speeds for hours. In a field that can consist of dozens of drivers, a loose brake line or a shaky call by a fatigued driver can cause a pileup, a crash, or even a death.

That's why the industry has built in several precautions. Some are technological. The wall on the track, known as a "soft wall," is made of foam and steel; it diffuses the impact when a car makes contact with it. The IndyCar driver wears a device that attaches the helmet to the back of the seat so that in the event of a crash his or her head will remain relatively stable. Other precautions involve the personal character of the team member. Most drivers are initially attracted to racing because they love exercising their courage, but unless they are also capable of exercising good judgment, they don't stick around long. The same goes for the team members; they are picked because they are skilled and levelheaded.

Yet great technology and great people aren't enough, not when very small errors can lead to terrible outcomes. Team members are taught to pay attention to the very faint signals that something could go wrong.

These signals start in the garage, where mechanics prepare the car. The cars are complicated, and the work is fast. If the wrong part is used, a car can become destabilized during the race. If the team's engineer wants a particular type of part—for example, a damper (shock absorber)—he begins a paper trail. He sends an order for the damper; the crew member who builds the damper then brings it, with the order, to the mechanics. The mechanics then install it. Along the way, each person signs the order. If a crew member receives a part without an order to go with it, he refuses to install the part. The paper trail—or lack of it—is investigated, to determine that the part in hand is indeed the part that is required. Later, during the race, the crew tracks the driver's decisions via sensors in the car and a communications system. If a driver shifts gears a little too early, or if he or she asks a question whose answer seems obvious, the crew takes note—even if the race is generally going favorably. The crew members increase communication and work to keep the tired driver focused.

Karl Weick, a psychologist at the University of Michigan's Ross School of Business, is an expert on the subject of mistakes. His research explores what he calls "high-reliability organizations" (HROs), such as aircraft carriers, air traffic controllers, nuclear power plants, and hospital emergency departments. For these organizations, like the IndyCar pit crews, even a small misstep can lead to death or disaster.

One of Weick's consistent findings is that HROs pay attention to faint warning signs, such as strain in a race car driver's voice, and correct problems early. Their attention to small mistakes is an antidote to the poison of perfectionism. In life-and-death pressure cookers like IndyCar racing, it would be easy for management to decree a ban on mistakes. Although it's necessary to expect staff members to bring their best efforts, a perfectionistic attitude does not prevent mistakes. It only drives those mistakes underground. When employees of a perfectionistic supervisor make errors, they will try to hide them, shift the blame, or tell themselves that the mistake isn't significant.

High-reliability organizations know they cannot afford to play games of secrecy. Their attention to small mistakes flows from the recognition that human beings, no matter how gifted, are fallible. Instead of expecting staff members to be perfect, HROs require them to be transparent. Weick relates a dramatic story of a mechanic on an aircraft carrier who could not locate one of his wrenches. A lost wrench hardly seems like an error of tragic proportions, but this is a U.S. Navy aircraft carrier we are speaking of.

Pilots take off and land their planes on its deck; one lapse could result in lost lives and millions of dollars in damage. In this case, the mechanic realized that if his wrench were laying somewhere on the deck, it could be sucked into an aircraft's engine, destroying both plane and pilot. He reported his problem to an officer, who canceled the day's maneuvers until the wandering wrench could be found. The next day, the mechanic received an award. The commanding officer used the lost-wrench episode to send a message to the entire crew: *If you make a mistake, tell us so that we can prevent a bigger problem.*[1] That message echoes a sign that W. Edwards Deming placed in his kaizen factories, in block letters: FIX THE PROBLEM, NOT THE BLAME.

Deming's sign underscores an essential element of HROs: they understand that a punitive, vengeful attitude toward mistakes runs counter to their mission. The Federal Aviation Association (FAA), where whip-smart employees facilitate the safe takeoffs and landings of several hundreds of thousands of flights every day, recognizes that pride and fear can inhibit staff from reporting their own errors. So the FAA set up a hotline that allows employees to report their errors discreetly. Anyone who reports his or her own mistakes will not be punished, although they may receive retraining if needed. But anyone who fails to report a mistake *will* receive a reprimand. And in HROs, managers make a point of talking about their own mistakes; they are modeling the honest, mindful attitude that they want their employees to adopt.

We can all apply high-reliability thinking to our work lives, looking for small mistakes and encouraging transparency. Sometimes all it takes to "see" errors is an examina-

The Spirit of Kaizen

tion of your conscience. What are you letting slide? What's been giving you a troubling sense that all is not well? But there are situations in which it's difficult for all of us to spot mistakes. Once you're aware of these mental blindfolds, you can lift them out of the way and make it easier to see mistakes.

MENTAL BLINDFOLD 1:
"BUT WE GET SO MANY THINGS RIGHT!"

When your company puts in a heroic performance on a daily basis, it's easy to ignore the rogue mistakes. You may recall the summer when an engineering flaw in the Bridgestone/Firestone tire, which was the standard tire for Ford's Explorer sports-utility vehicle, led to 80 rollovers and more than 100 deaths. Bridgestone/Firestone seemed to have let the scope of its production blind it to the disaster's significance. When the company responded to deaths, it pointed out that during the period when those 80 tires failed, they had manufactured more than 14 million tires that performed perfectly. The response was statistically true, but it was not useful. Customers hardly felt reassured knowing that there was only a *small* chance of dying while using the company's product.

Better to follow the example set by FedEx, which likes to remind its employees that the company's goal is to provide excellent service *every day*. FedEx avoids falling into the trap of thinking, "Hey, we do we amazingly well *most* of the time," by putting their numbers into the context of customer service. They acknowledge to their employees that a 99 percent success rate sounds impressive. But if FedEx delivers 3 million packages a night and only succeeds 99 percent of the time, there are 30 thousand customers who will be disappointed *each night*.[2] Emphasizing the numbers in the negative direction is an effective way of making the point.

MENTAL BLINDFOLD 2: DON'T MESS WITH SUCCESS

As a business succeeds, it tends to engender a worshipful attitude toward its institutional procedures and people. After all, these are the factors that brought the business its fortune. In these businesses, it's heresy to speak up when a system is no longer working optimally, or when a longtime manager has made a misstep. That's too bad, because those glossed-over mistakes are the seedbeds of irrelevance. They are lost chances to sharpen, to focus, and to remain competitive.

Avoiding this don't-mess-with-success mentality is a centerpiece of Pixar's preservice training. Pixar's management makes a point of acknowledging to new hires that joining a successful organization, especially one that has a long string of commercial and critical successes, can be intimidating. Management then explains that Pixar relies on its new employees to continue its history of success—not by merely repeating what has worked before but by bringing their suggestions, complaints, concerns, and questions out in the open. This mindset is reinforced at the completion of each film, when everyone is gathered together to list five things that worked well in the movie and five things that need to be improved. The encouraging message? Nothing here is ever perfect, yet we strive for perfection.

MENTAL BLINDFOLD 3: NO NEWS IS GOOD NEWS

If your employees insist that there are no problems you need to know about, consider their confidence a red flag, especially if you are in a corporate culture that has historically denied or punished mistakes. When Alan Mulally stepped in as president and CEO of the Ford Motor Corporation in 2006, the company was deep in the red. One of Mulally's first moves was to meet with the managers of each division. He gave them a series of cards designed to report the condition of their product. A green card meant everything was going well. A yellow card indicated that the department suffered from a few issues. A red card signified major problems requiring immediate attention. When Mulally asked the managers to hold up the appropriate card, every single one was green.

Mulally was stunned. He explained to his staff that since Ford was losing billions of dollars, there was no way that all its systems were running smoothly. In essence, he gave them permission to be honest. At the next meeting, he asked again for a show of cards; one brave soul held up a red one. Mulally applauded with approval. Other people at the meeting, feeling less frightened, helped forge a solution to the red-card problem. The next week, to use Mulally's words, he asked for cards and he "saw a rainbow."[3]

Recall the original *Star Wars* movie? When director George Lucas had Darth Vader telepathically asphyxiate staff members who reported bad news, he was channeling the anxieties of middle managers everywhere. He knew that people are terrified of telling the truth to their bosses. That's why, if you want to know what's *really* going on in your work world, you must be prepared to react positively and energetically the instant an employee admits to a problem. You don't have to applaud, as Alan Mulally did, but you could say something like, "I know it took courage for you to tell me about this problem" or "I'm glad you told me."

If you take an encouraging tone toward small mistakes but you still don't hear about them, you can actively look for them. Try letting one particular small mistake serve as your company's canary in the coal mine, a signal that something more serious may be wrong. A clever example comes from an unusual source: the rock band Van Halen. David Lee Roth, the lead singer of Van Halen, was notorious for insisting that concert promoters provide him with a bowl of M&Ms in his backstage suite, with all the brown M&Ms removed. This request was written into each of Van Halen's contracts, which stipulated that if the condition was not met, the concert could be canceled but the promoter would still owe Van Halen its payment in full. What appeared to be a rock star's petulance was, in fact, a kaizen approach to preventing mistakes. As David Lee Roth explained in his book, *Crazy from the Heat*, his band's show was more complex than others of the time; whereas most bands arrived at a concert venue with three trucks loaded with gear, Van Halen pulled up with nine eighteen-wheelers. After a few shows that were riddled with technical errors, Roth devised his M&M scheme. Placing a high value on a detail as small as the color of a candy, he reasoned, would put the promoter on notice: *everything* about this show was important. And Roth now had a simple way to gauge the potential for larger errors. "When I would walk backstage," he says, "if I saw a brown M&M in that bowl, well, we'd line-check the entire production. Guaranteed you're going to arrive at a technical error. Guaranteed you'd run into a problem."[4]

MENTAL BLINDFOLD 4:
WE'RE TOO SMART TO MAKE MISTAKES

A kaizen presumption is that human beings will make mistakes. And when you assume that humans are fallible, the next logical question becomes this: How do you build systems that compensate for the likelihood of error?

The airline industry has taken this question to heart. Say what you will about bad food and delays, airlines are one of the miracles of modern life. A commercial airplane is made from more than 1 million components, and each is a variable that increases the odds that something will go awry. Yet all over the planet, several hundred thousands of flights take off and land safely every day. This high rate of reliability occurs not because airline employees are perfect but because the airline industry is built on the assumption that human beings will screw up anything they touch. Instead of relying on their memory, pilots use checklists to make sure the doors are secure, all circuits are switched to their correct positions, and even that their lap straps are tight. As a passenger, I once abandoned the in-flight movie and listened to a different channel, the one that lets passengers hear conversations between the pilots and air traffic controllers. I heard the controller issue instructions to the pilot about speed and altitude; the communication was short and clear. What happened next was critical: *The pilot repeated back what he had heard.* The industry assumes that air traffic controllers sometimes misspeak and pilots sometimes don't listen; repeating the words allows both parties to confirm the message.

Compare the safety statistics of the airline industry, in which the chance of any one person dying in a U.S. domestic flight is 1 in 60 million,[5] with the medical world's, in which 98 thousand deaths are attributed to human error each year. Instead of recognizing that humans are error-prone, the health-care industry trusts that its employees will perform flawlessly—that they will always flip the right switch, read a chart correctly, and listen without being distracted. As a result, the airline industry has more safeguards against error than hospitals do. In particular, medical-safety experts have pleaded for standardized tube sizes or colors, so that feeding tubes, say, are easily distinguished from tubes that attach to intravenous lines. While the statistics for intubation errors are not reported by any agency, a 2006 survey reported that 16 percent of hospitals reported having confused feeding tubes with tubes meant for another part of the body. Standardized sizes would allow nurses to identify the appropriate tubing in much the same way that standardized sizes for gasoline and die-scl fuels prevent gas-station customers from putting the wrong fuel into their cars. It would be far better for the industry—and its patients—if it could build in systems that account for the ways that even the smartest and most focused professionals can go wrong.[6]

改

MENTAL BLINDFOLD 5: EVERYONE IS RESPONSIBLE

Dr. W. Edwards Deming was once approached by a head of accounting who was quite frustrated. The accountant complained that employees' time cards often contained mistakes: hours didn't add up, days were missing, and so on. It was a small issue, but correcting those errors was an added expense to the accounting department.

Deming asked to see the time card. At the top was a line for the employees' name and signature, followed by spaces to mark the number of hours worked. At the bottom was a line for the supervisor's signature. Deming held the card for a minute, studied it, erased the line at the bottom, and handed it back to the accountant.

Asking two people to share responsibility for a problem is a bad idea. In this case, neither the employees nor the supervisors really "saw" the mistakes. The employees thought: *It doesn't really matter what I do with these cards. The supervisor will double-check it before signing off.* The supervisors thought: *My employees will fill these out fairly accurately; all I need to do is give the card a brief glance.* When the employee was put in charge, the problem disappeared.

MENTAL BLINDFOLD 6:
RUSH TO MARKET

When you have a new product or service, beating your competitors to the market may feel like a top priority. Small problems look like speed bumps, and staff members are encouraged to power over them. But being first is not the same as being best. Many iconic firms were not the original producers of an idea; they learned from the mistakes of the first and then developed a superior product. Apple didn't invent a single category of product. Southwest Airlines didn't invent low-cost fares. Google didn't invent search engines. McDonald's didn't invent the fast-food burger.

In haste to reach the goal of being first or biggest, companies can make terrible mistakes. An example is Toyota, one of the companies that embraced the kaizen philosophy following World War II. For 60 years, Toyota carefully nurtured its reputation for excellence. Using a practice called *jojo*, which means "slowly, gradually, and steadily," the company expanded—but it did so at a measured, deliberate pace, in order to ensure that quality would not be jeopardized. Toyota's reputation was unimpeachable. Even *Consumer Reports* used to endorse Toyota's cars without test-driving them first.

Then a new management team came on the scene and declared that Toyota would soon become the world's *biggest* auto manufacturer. In their haste to achieve this goal, they expanded at a furious pace, opening two factories every year—even though they often lacked the engineering support to assure their standards of quality. They no longer had time to carefully instruct suppliers in Toyota's precise methods. They stopped examining defects that showed up in cars after their warranties had expired. In the midst of this process, Toyota's head of human resources, Teruo Suzuki, stated prophetically, "We make so many cars in so many different places with so many people. Our greatest fear is that as we keep growing, our ability to maintain the discipline of *kaizen* will be lost."[7]

Unfortunately, that discipline did seem to be lost. In 2009, Toyota began what would become a series of major recalls of its cars for flaws that included unintended acceleration. By 2011, Toyota—its reputation in shreds—had recalled more than 9 million cars.

As Steven Spear, a Massachusetts Institute of Technology operations expert, has commented, "If quality is first, it drives a certain set of behaviors. If market share is the goal, it drives a different set of behaviors. Even in the late 1990s, people in Toyota would say, 'This is going to bite us in the ass.' They just didn't know when."

LET MISTAKES CHANGE YOUR CRITERIA FOR SUCCESS OR FAILURE

Once you have improved your ability to see small mistakes, make it known that you expect everyone in the company to see them, too—and to offer solutions. One railroad used this tactic when it was suffering from an on-time performance of 80 percent, far short of what the CEO and the customers wanted. The company tried using innovation to solve the problem. Its executives hired more staff and improved their traffic-control systems, but neither of these expensive interventions did the trick.

Then they took a kaizen approach. They noticed that when a unit of the railroad experienced a problem that could lead to a delay, one of the other units often had the resources to solve the problem. But one unit rarely stepped in to help another; thus, delays were born.

The company changed its procedure. If one unit had a problem that it could not solve on its own, it had to ask for help from a second unit. If the second unit refused, it—not the first unit—was assigned the blame for the delay. With this very simple step, both large and small mistakes were communicated and solved much more efficiently. Within four months, the railroad's on-time performance rate soared to 98 percent.[8] More important, the company had changed its definition of success. It was no longer enough to put your head down and do your job. Now, helping other employees was a measure of your success or failure.

This strategy is pure kaizen. Kaizen companies do not expect quality to be the province of a few experts who stand at the end of the line and review the day's work. Kaizen insists that *everyone* in an organization is responsible for quality to the same degree. It is the responsibility of management to make it as easy as possible for ideas and suggestions to flow from the bottom and from the middle toward the people who need them. When necessary, those ideas should have a clear path all the way up to the top.

改

Kaizen Pathway: Mistake Policy

改善

When I begin working with an organization, one of the first questions I ask is, "What is your policy for dealing with mistakes?" The client is often startled at first, but quickly sees the point. If you pretend that mistakes don't or shouldn't happen in your organization, you are making a grave error yourself. Here are some questions that can lead to a mistake policy in your department or company:

1. Define the mistakes your organization wants to avoid at all costs. (Of course, some mistakes can be creative and useful; I'll talk about these in Chapter 5, "Develop New Products and Services.")

2. Share these mistakes with your team. Put your heads together and figure out what the earliest warning signs of these mistakes look like. Emphasize the importance of watching out for faint signals of big problems.

3. Ask your staff: Where are the O-rings? (Scorched O-rings were the earliest warning signs of the problems leading to the *Challenger* disaster.) That is, where are the

mistakes that are being ignored because no one wants to see them?

4. Decide how you'll make it safe for employees to talk about errors. How will you extract the lesson from the mistake and share it with the larger group?

善

Chapter Five

DEVELOP
NEW PRODUCTS
AND SERVICES

*A common misperception about
kaizen is that small steps always
lead to small results. But this
is simply not true. Kaizen steps
can lead to inventions that
change the world.*

Are you curious? Are you sure?

Most people believe they are curious
because they sometimes ask questions. The
accountant, the doctor, the lawyer, and the
parent all ask questions . . . but the purpose
of most questions is to elicit specific information in order to achieve a solution. That's an

important skill, but it's not curiosity. It's problem solving. Curiosity is the ability to engage your interest in whatever is happening at the moment, no matter whether the moment is large or small, dramatic or tedious, pleasant or painful. And it's curiosity that leads to the inventions—the new products and services—that an organization needs if it is to grow and stay competitive.

改

Have you ever noticed how creativity is portrayed on movies or television? Usually, the creative person faces a problem—a blank canvas, for example, or a fresh sheet of paper—and stares it down, hands on hips, face arranged in a thoughtful expression. Then his body sags. He might sit down, his head in his hands. He bangs his head against the back of the chair for a while. He may pour a drink. A colleague says, "You know what the matter is? You're working too hard." He goes for a walk in the twilight. He stands in front of the canvas or paper some more, this time at different angles. He sits again and sighs. And then . . . inspiration! He gets to work, animated by his revolutionary vision.

A pleasure of watching movies and TV shows is that they reshape reality into an elegant package—but be careful. Even the best biographical films use fictional techniques to represent the creative process. Why? Because true creativity doesn't make a great story.

Inspiration is much more likely to develop from the habit of consistently paying attention to life's *small* moments. I first understood this fact when I was a graduate student in psychology. I learned about mental disorders and the darker aspects of the mind, but I also wanted to understand success. How do people solve problems? How do they overcome obstacles? What happens to make people see life in a new or particularly useful way?

One way I approached these questions was to examine some of history's worst problems and how people generated solutions. It didn't take long for me to focus on plagues, which are one of the great terrors of humanity; throughout history, plagues have killed hundreds of millions of people. Smallpox in particular has a satisfying narrative because it had such terrible consequences—severe disfiguration and a mortality rate of about 30 percent—and a precise ending, which came in 1979, when the World Health Organization declared the disease eradicated. It was Dr. Edward Jenner who, in the late 1800s, took us down the path to this happy conclusion, surely one of humanity's biggest wins. By this time, I was already suspicious of the "bolt of inspiration" theory of creativity. I imagined that Jenner's work on smallpox featured a careful application of the most advanced medical thinking and specialized technology available. I hypothesized that he might have traveled from one wise medical man to another, learning their secrets, working up variations of their ideas until one stuck. I was wrong.

Jenner's most creative thinking about smallpox was generated by a conversation with a milkmaid. "I shall never have smallpox," the woman told him, "for I have had cowpox. I shall never have an ugly pockmarked face." Was this a crucial bit of insider information that led the lucky Jenner to the connection between the two diseases? No. Everyone, including other scientists seeking a smallpox cure, knew that milkmaids were far less likely to get smallpox than people in other occupations. But the information was so ordinary, so commonplace, that no one really understood that it held a critical clue. It was Jenner who recognized its value. He realized that the less-dangerous cowpox virus might confer immunity against smallpox, and those observations helped him create a smallpox vaccine. Was Jenner more fired up, more inspired, and more innovative than other scientists of the time? Maybe yes and maybe no. A more useful observation is that Jenner was more willing to pay attention to the commonplace.

Creativity is not a cloud, a bolt, or an electric spark. It does not descend upon you as you sit more or less passively in your chair, discontentedly awaiting its arrival as you pound your forehead with your fist. Creativity is not a *thing*. It's an activity. It is the attention to life's "insignificant" moments that can lead to successful changes, services, and products. In Jenner's case, it was the attention to small talk with a milkmaid—the kind of conversation every doctor of the era probably had at some point—of asking the milkmaid a question, listening to the answer, and following up with new questions to himself. Perhaps those questions went something like: *What are the similarities between cowpox and smallpox? What are the differences? Are there other diseases that share similarities, and what do we know about them?*

Although you can practice creativity at any time, there are certain moments that tend to be especially fruitful for producing ideas. Like Jenner, you can look for moments that everyone else takes for granted. Here are a few other flavors of creative opportunity:

- *Embarrassment*. When people are embarrassed, it's because there's a gap between what they feel they

should have done and what they actually did. Embarrassment is an intensely uncomfortable feeling. It's instinctive to avoid it by covering up the mistake or even trying to hide from the people who might have heard about it. Even the more mature among us, who will own up to our errors and correct our mistakes, and maybe even laugh at ourselves, will seek to move on as quickly as possible.

What if you try a different tactic? What if you stare down into that dark gap between what was supposed to happen and what really took place? What if you look for unexamined assumptions or strange new forms of knowledge that you can bring to light?

One of my favorite examples of creative embarrassment comes from the labs of Queen Elizabeth College in London, where the chemist Shashikant Phadnis was working on a substance he presumed would act as a new, improved insecticide. He'd been told to test the chemical, but he misunderstood the instruction and thought he'd been asked to taste it. When his supervisor found out that Phadnis had put the chemical in his mouth, he thought Phadnis was crazy. The story could easily have ended there, as a funny anecdote about office life, one that Phadnis might have been eager for everyone to forget. But Phadnis saw possibility. A year later, after multiple experiments resulting from the accidental taste test, the lab invented Splenda, the best-selling sweetener. (The inventions of Sweet'N Low and Equal were also the results of accidents that happened to intrigue investigators.)[1]

- *Wastefulness.* When time is wasted or an item is broken, you can lose your temper. You can replace the item or reconfigure your schedule. Or you can act with curiosity.

    When you act with curiosity, you may ask yourself something like this: *How can I prevent this waste from happening again?* In 1892, James C. Fargo visited Europe on vacation. Even though he was the head of American Express—then an express mail business—and carried personal letters of credit, he had trouble getting banks to give him cash. The letters of credit, and the effort it had taken to secure them, were wasted. Fargo complained, "The moment I got off the beaten track they were no more useful than so much wet wrapping paper." This frustration led to the invention of the Travelers Cheque.[2] You might say that a dislike of wastefulness is the mother of invention.

    There's another way to respond to waste. Perry Spencer, an engineer at Raytheon, lost his chocolate candy bar when he left it near a piece of radar equipment and it started to melt. It's easy to imagine a busy engineer thinking:, *Oh, great. Of course radar would heat up chocolate, I should have known . . . a* *I was so hungry, too. Well, clean up the mess an* *over it, buddy. Back to work.* Instead Spencer ' curious and began to investigate the possi⊢ curiosity led him to invent the microw·

- *Silly problems.* We all yearn for signif· times this longing can get twisted '

attractive: self-importance. Self-importance takes the form of dismissing other people's problems as silly or trivial. Self-importance says: *I'm busy trying to solve big problems. I don't have time for you and your pale little life, because I'm feeding the world/building a rocket/mathematically proving the existence of perfect cuboids!* Self-importance usually leads to sitting alone in your office, waiting for an idea that is worthy of your genius, and wondering why no one wants to talk to you anymore.

True inventiveness occurs when the inventor cares about little problems. The Post-it note was famously invented when a 3M employee, Arthur Fry, was struggling to mark songs in his hymnal

Sometimes there is an intersection between inventiveness and consideration: Earle Dickson, an employee of Johnson & Johnson, wanted to help his wife, who frequently cut herself while preparing dinner. It took a few false starts, but he created a ready-to-use bandage to help stop the bleeding and make it less likely that the wound would reopen. The Band-Aid brand adhesive bandage not only worked for Dickson's wife, it became Johnson & Johnson's most successful product.[4] And Ikea began developing customer-assembled furniture after a photographer noticed how much trouble it took to load traditional furniture onto a truck after a photo shoot.[5]

- *Boredom.* One of Walt Disney's most spectacular creations, Disneyland, was born from a moment of attentive boredom. Disney had taken his two young daughters to an amusement park. He placed them on a ride and sat on a bench until the ride was over. At the end of the ride, he collected the children, took them to a second ride and sat on a second bench. Sitting on the third bench, he was bored—obviously!—but he pursued that feeling with interest. There must be, he decided, a way for a family to share an amusement park together. Disneyland was invented on that third bench.[6] And listlessness during an airplane ride gave Robert Worsley the idea for *Skymall* magazine; he turned boredom into an opportunity to get some shopping done.[7]

What a relief to know that creativity doesn't require any special talent; it only requires attention. You can practice the mental discipline that it takes to be focused and inquisitive, even when life isn't particularly glorious or supersized. Kaizen steps can help you cultivate attentiveness and grow the most basic kinds of curiosity.

TRAIN YOURSELF IN THE CURIOSITY RESPONSE

Some of the best products and services are invented when people respond to stressful moments—moments that are tedious, embarrassing, tense, or painful in some other way—with curiosity. Yet curiosity is not an instinctive response to pain. When the amygdala—recall that this is the brain's alarm center—is activated by stress, the brain is flooded with anger and worry, and the creative cortex is compromised or completely shut down.

You can learn to react differently to stress, to replace the amygdala's alarm bells with curiosity. Just as pilots use simulators to unlearn their panic reaction to wind shear and replace it with a series of trained responses, you can rehearse using your curiosity in times of stress. You do this by putting yourself in the stressful position of talking to a person who pushes your hot buttons. In a safe, nonbusiness setting, seek out conversations with people whose opinions are different from yours. Don't try to persuade, cajole, or demonstrate your superiority to the other person; instead, ask questions that are open-ended and imply no judgment or opinion. Gather information. Adopt an attitude of curiosity.

I had an opportunity to practice my curiosity response a short time ago, when I boarded an airplane for a long flight and found myself seated next to a woman eager for conversation. Fine by me, except that she wanted to talk about her love of hunting. That would have been all right with me, too—but this woman loved to hunt big African animals, just for the sport of it. I felt uncomfortable with her activities and with her blithe attitude. It was a perfect opportunity to overcome my rising stress levels and ask questions. Note that I restrained myself from asking peevish questions like, "So do you get a thrill out of killing endangered animals?" Instead, I tried these questions:

> *How did you become interested in hunting?*
> *What are the challenges of hunting?*
> *What do you enjoy the most about hunting?*
> *How did you learn to hunt?*
> *When did you start hunting?*

She responded with enthusiasm—and, oddly enough, so did I. She didn't convert me to her philosophy, but I did appreciate her excitement. And I made the discovery that hunting was only one chapter in my seatmate's vigorous life. The 30 minutes I spent replacing my distress with curiosity will make it easier for me to draw on this skill later, when I face challenges that are much more upsetting to me.

Other neutral questions to ask when you are feeling angered, frightened, or stressed-out include:

Can you help me understand more about . . . ?

What are your thoughts about . . . ?

What would you suggest I tell people when they state that . . . ?

What convinced you of this path/belief/point of view?

Can you tell me more about . . . ?

CROSS-COLLABORATE

Think of how water is made: molecules of hydrogen crash into molecules of oxygen. Creativity sometimes works like this, too, when one person's way of thinking bumps into another's. Old ways of thinking break apart; ideas float free and attach themselves to pieces of other ideas, making themselves into new shapes.

Decades ago, when men ran the businesses but women ran the parties where business got done, it was the hostesses who knew how to set the stage for creative collaboration. A successful hostess once told me the secret to a brilliant party. Naïvely, I thought she'd produce a spectacular recipe or share a secret for floral arrangements. But her advice spoke directly to creative psychology: "Invite people who don't know one another very well, put them together around a dinner table that is slightly too small, and give them food that is easy to like and easy to eat." "Oh," she said, "and turn down the heat."

I asked her to explain this unusual "recipe" for a good party. She told me that if people were just a little bit chilly, they would unconsciously turn to their dinner companions for warmth—leaning in to hear the conversation or nudging with an elbow. If the table was small, it was all the more likely to promote a lively mix of ideas and information.

If you want to encourage creativity among your staff, a simple kaizen step is to learn from this hostess and make collaboration a physical event. Companies like Pixar and Google put people with different specialties in the same room to maximize the opportunities for pollinating ideas. Tom Kelley of IDEO, the design and innovation consulting firm, recommends small, cramped spaces to maximize interactions.[8]

Bell Labs, which for a good part of the twentieth century was one of the world's most creative organizations, took a different approach. One of its buildings included hallways so long that you could stand at the beginning of one end and not see all the way to the other end. The idea, reports Jon Gertner in the *New York Times*, was to mix up the brain power that was sitting inside the hall's offices: "Traveling down the hall's length without encountering a number of acquaintances, problems, diversions, and ideas was almost impossible. A physicist on his way to lunch in the cafeteria was like a magnet rolling past iron fillings."[9]

Even a very small change can promote creative chance and connections. When a European IT firm's management wanted to design their new offices to foster cross-collaboration, they asked me to help. They were stymied. In their current space, they'd tried making the coffee room large and comfortable but then discovered that employees were reticent to use it; they feared others would see them and think they weren't working very hard. Management took down inner walls, creating a large open space where people could see one another. This step was even less popular. Some employees had loud telephone voices that distracted the others; people felt they had no control over interruptions by well-meaning colleagues. Exhausted from the time and expense of these changes, the firm's management wanted to give kaizen a try.

First, I conducted a brief survey of the employees, asking who was considered the most creative and productive. (I assured the employees that I would not announce the results; nor would I inform management.) I then unobtrusively observed the top five employees as they migrated through the office space during a workday. I was delighted and surprised to discover that there was already a physical space where these five met up and briefly exchanged ideas and information: the copy machine. In retrospect, the copy machine is an obvious meeting place. Everyone is working (unlike in the coffee break room), either making copies or waiting to make copies. People don't have to worry about interruptions or extended visits. After all, they just came to make copies.

We designed the new offices so that all of the copy machines were located *between* departments, so that every employee would be drawn into this pattern of exchange. A few people complained about having to walk farther, but I explained the kaizen health benefits of taking a few more steps each day. (For more on this topic, see Chapter 7, "Reduce Health-Care Costs.") Surveys taken six months later revealed higher levels of understanding of the roles of other departments and increased collaboration across the organization. Another survey, taken one month before the move, showed that only 12 percent of employees sat with staff from other departments. Three months after the move, interdepartment seating went up to 44 percent. All of these changes resulted from moving a few copy machines.

RESOLVE THE MISTAKE PARADOX

Another kaizen strategy for increasing creativity is to attend carefully to mistakes. I've already described the importance of correcting errors while they are still embryonic, but merely correcting errors is a management misstep in itself. The paradox of mistakes is as follows:

> *We all know that innovation requires trial-and-error learning and making mistakes.*
>
> *Nobody likes making mistakes.*

The way to resolve this paradox is to create small pilot experiments that encourage mistakes within a contained environment, one that allows for learning while minimizing costs. Effective leaders encourage people to take small, educated risks and to report the results. These leaders make a point of rewarding admissions of error; they know that a small but "failed" experiment pays off with information and insight at a minimal cost.

When a pilot project fails at 3M, the staff sets off a small cannon and has a party. When the German scientist Wernher von Braun was told of a programming mistake during the development of the Redstone missile, he sent the engineer a bottle of Champagne.[10] The admission spared the government expensive tests and made the corrections simpler.

Jeff Bezos, the CEO of Amazon, takes a similar approach. "I encourage our employees to go down blind alleys and experiment. If we can get processes decentralized so that we can do a lot of experiments without it being very costly, we'll get a lot more innovation."[11]

Even more rewarding is when small pilot projects directly fuel success. When consulting with a software company, I was invited to attend its regional meeting. The CEO introduced a new software project that she thought would be a hit. The organization was a healthy one, and several members of the sales staff were comfortable enough to express their skepticism. They liked the product well enough but thought that customers might not be willing to pay for it. The CEO handled the feedback beautifully. She told the salespeople that they might be right, and she suggested that they find one or two teams in different states to test customer response.

I immediately thought of something a Toyota marketing director told me. The great Eiji Toyoda, the company's former chairman and president, dreamed of making a luxury car with the quietest engine he could imagine. He shared the specifications of this dream car with his chief engineer, who quickly told him it was impossible. No engine could meet those demands; even if it could, the cost would be enormous. According to the marketing director, Toyoda quietly requested "Please, build me just one." The result, eventually, was the Lexus.

The software company's CEO was similarly persistent—but her lack of defensiveness and her interest in a small experiment reduced the sales staff's fear of wasting a lot of time, energy, and financial resources in a difficult market. Two small teams volunteered, and within a month, the company's intranet was buzzing about the customers' enthusiastic response. At this point, the product could have been described as an initial success.

The CEO then wisely sent out an e-mail, announcing that the two small teams had provided encouraging news . . . but that instead of rolling out the product throughout the company, she would gather more data by asking for two more teams to volunteer. In addition, she asked the two initial teams to discuss the sales strategies they'd found useful. This way, she allowed the teams to *share in* the success, and she ensured that the second phase of the experiment could build on the first. By the time the two additional teams reported their good results, the rest of the sales force was ready to sign on; their fears had been respected and tested, data had been gathered, and a solid strategy had been developed. After the successful national launch of the software, the CEO sent a message to the sales staff. "Thank you," she said, "to those of you who raised concerns, and thank you to the sales staff who volunteered to investigate by calling on customers." Her words and actions were the model of openness and responsiveness. It is these qualities that reduce fear and allow creativity to flow.

改

PATIENCE, THE COUSIN OF CREATIVITY

A close cousin of creativity is patience. As we enjoy the benefits of other people's creativity, from great inventions to great novels, we are seldom aware of the lengths of gestation that they required. We assume as we see the impressive results that the process was one of big, sudden steps that quickly reached fruition, fame, and fortune. The actual process is often much slower:

- *Einstein's theory of relativity.* It took 10 years to complete. There was no single "Eureka!" moment when the mystery of the universe whipped off its shiny wrapping and offered itself to Einstein like a present.

- *James Joyce's literary masterpiece*, Ulysses. It also took 10 years to write. Joyce is infamous for insisting that a properly thoughtful reading of his book should take 10 years too.

- *Henry Ford's Model T.* It was named after the twentieth letter of the alphabet. Why? Because Ford developed and rejected 19 automobiles before he arrived at one that was successful.

To labor for so long at projects the world is not asking for—or that it wants done yesterday—demands a particularly firm-minded brand of patience. It requires the belief that your actions will be worthwhile, even in the absence of any evidence.

I see the power of patience when a truly wise leader is confronting major challenges. It takes enormous discipline to withstand the pressure to take large, dramatic steps that merely give the appearance that big things are happening. Taking the time to listen, to understand, and to try small steps first requires faith that the accumulation of small steps may lead to big improvements.

I have watched clients eager to invent "the next big thing" try creativity workshops or brainstorming sessions with hundreds or even thousands of people. The workshops can be enjoyable, but when the client returns he or she is still the same person—and is still too harried to lay the groundwork for creativity. The result is often discouragement and despair.

The relatively rare person will patiently commit to a modest program of attention, questioning, and experimenting, making a few changes each day. The slow, steady positive increase in creative thought builds confidence and commitment, and usually leads to ideas that can be applied in the service of the organization.

ASK SMALL QUESTIONS

For reasons that nobody truly understands, the brain cannot reject small questions. Any small question, especially one you ask repeatedly, prompts your brain to begin its own Google search.

I sometimes offer multiday kaizen seminars at hotels and spas, and use the occasion to demonstrate the odd power of small questions. I ask, "How many of you walked to this event room from your hotel?" Almost everyone raises a hand. "OK," I say, "How many statues are on the path between the hotel and the event suite?" They always look at one another, as if to say, *This man is an idiot*, but they have to admit they have no answer. I leave the topic alone until the opening of the next day's sessions, when I ask it again. By the final day, even though the audience has far more interesting and important things on their mind, they find that they can answer my question and tell me exactly how many statues line the path.

It's a ridiculous question, and that's what makes it so effective. No matter what the topic, the brain is compelled to pay attention to small questions. You can try to command your brain—*Pay attention to the statues!*—but it's much less effective. Your brain doesn't like being barked at. It will, in essence, fold its arms and refuse to budge, much like a stubborn child who doesn't want to put away his toys.

Ironically, the smaller the question, the more likely you are to get an answer. A large question such as, "How can I reduce payroll by 20 percent?" has a paralyzing effect. Large questions turn on the fear response, alert the amygdala, and shut down the cerebral cortex. But if the question is small, the amygdala stays quiet, unthreatened. Ask the question repeatedly, and the brain absorbs the question without getting overwhelmed. And in its own magical way, it will eventually pop out an answer.

If you want to come up with a new product or service, it's best to:

- Avoid commands.

  Come up with something good! Now!

- Avoid large questions.

  What is something brilliant that my company could offer the world?

- Avoid self-recrimination disguised as a question.

  Why can't you ever come up with a good idea, you moron?

Instead, it's best to ask very small questions like these.

- What is the smallest way we could improve one of our products?

- What is a small but annoying problem that affects our customers?

- Is there one change that would make the day easier for my spouse, neighbor, colleague, or customer?

- Is there something that embarrassed me today? Bored me? Wasted my time?

- Was there anything in those situations that I could learn from?"

Don't expect an answer to come to you right away. Be patient. Continue to ask the question, and allow your brain to enjoy the challenge. When it is ready, you'll receive an answer.

Chapter Six

INCREASE
SALES

Even for the best salespeople, the act of selling can be intimidating or demoralizing. Conventional wisdom tries to inspire or invigorate salespeople out of their fear, but kaizen dismantles fear by taking an easy, calm path around it.

Selling is scary. This is true, no more matter how you define "sales." For our purposes, I'll define sales broadly. It's an act of persuasion that encourages other people to exchange their money for your goods and services or to lend their support to your idea. Sales activities include:

- Selling sweaters at a Gap store.
- Pitching a proposal to some prospective clients.
- "Selling" your company to shareholders during a speech.
- Making cold calls to sell a product or fund-raise for an organization.

改

All of these activities are tailor-made to produce fear. Salespeople offer themselves and their products to the world, and more often than not the world responds with rejection or even rudeness. For a fortunate few, preparing for a sales call (or pitching a proposal, or approaching a customer who is standing in front of a sweater display) is like going up the first steep hill of a roller coaster. It's a moment of anticipation before the delirious thrill of plunging into the fast-on-your-feet activity of sales work.

For the rest of us, there's kaizen.

The majority of salespeople don't enjoy the fear, a fact made plain by the high turnover rate in sales departments. Kaizen is an ideal tool for training and retaining sales personnel, because it's perfect for frightening situations. Most of us are programmed to mentally shut down in a scary situation. This doesn't make us poor salespeople. We are simply responding to physiology. Recall how the brain responds to fear: when we are faced with a challenge that we feel is serious, the amygdala senses a threat to our survival. Like a bouncer at a trendy nightclub, the amygdala muscles past the rest of the brain and takes charge. It sends our classy, well-dressed intentions out the door. It orders our mental processes to slow down. Sometimes the amygdala sends messages telling us to face the danger directly, but most of the time it shouts, "Everybody! Run to the basement for safety until the danger is past!"

Yes, you can choose to hire only those salespeople whose brains naturally relish the excitement of a sale. But these people tend to burn out quickly. Training a sales staff can be expensive, and dropouts are costly and inefficient. Why not teach *all* of your salespeople a strategy for managing their fear? This is the kaizen method of moving past fear, one small step at a time. Imagine that fear is a lion standing between an employee and the sale. Kaizen doesn't rush at the lion. Kaizen sings the lion to sleep and then pads softly, quietly past the lion.

Instead of asking employees to make a big change to the way they act, encourage them to make small changes in the way they *think*. These kaizen steps include:

- Changing the way they talk to themselves.
- Changing the way they imagine the sale.
- Connecting their sales to a greater mission.

THINK SMALL THOUGHTS

I once worked with an insurance company that wanted to reduce turnover in its sales force. I interviewed both successful sales staff and the dropouts, and these conversations reminded me of the definition of self-esteem provided by the psychologist Martin Seligman: It's what you say to yourself when things are not going well. Successful salespeople have different internal conversations than the drop-outs when hearing the inevitable "no." The dropouts were quickly discouraged and heard an inner voice that said:

> "This is way too hard."
>
> "What is wrong with these people?"
>
> "I don't like this!"
>
> "Why am I such a failure?"

改

The successful salespeople who had endured rejections had very different inner conversations. Their voices were realistic but also confident:

> "I am offering customers a product (or service) that I believe in."
>
> "Every no gets me closer to a yes."
>
> "I am planting seeds for future sales."
>
> "This is a hard job that only strong people can do."

One possible solution was to whip the salespeople into a state of inspiration. This is what many companies do; they bring in a gifted and expensive motivational speaker, who ignites a fire in the audience. Another frequent strategy is to offer incentives. Of course, most salespeople receive commissions, but incentives usually go above and beyond the usual compensation and promise fancy trips or cars to the person with the biggest sales numbers. These approaches often work, but only temporarily. The memory of the inspirational speech fades away, or the staff members realize that even the big prizes don't help them handle the pain of being rejected over and over and over. Instead, I suggested a kaizen solution of focusing on "small thoughts"—on helping people find their way toward a few small changes in the words that were running in a loop through their mind.

This kaizen step took one hour. This was the time I carved out of the training to teach the salespeople about inner conversations. They listened and rehearsed what they wanted to say to themselves when the "no's" started piling up. Some latched onto the idea immediately. Others tried to imagine speaking to themselves kindly after a rejection . . . but sputtered. They rejected the encouraging statements as false. "They're platitudes," one pointed out. "They're just not true, at least not for me."

The struggling staff members tended to speak very harshly to themselves. Paradoxically, most people who beat themselves up are often quite thoughtful toward others. For this reason, people who can't imagine encouraging themselves can try a different approach: they can imagine that they are encouraging someone else who is frustrated and ready to give up. "What would you say to another salesperson who had been rejected?" I asked the trainees. "What tone of voice would you use?" This time, the answers flowed more readily:

> *Keep going. I know you can do this.*
>
> *With practice, you'll get better and better.*
>
> *You are selling a valuable product [or service] that can help your customer solve a problem.*
>
> *It takes courage to do what you do.*

Once the salespeople were satisfied with the encouraging words, I asked them to practice the phrases *out loud* once a day. I explained that the brain uses repetition as a major criterion for what it stores and builds into its neural networks. The brain commits cells and nerve pathways to the skills you are rehearsing. As the pathways become stronger, the initially awkward behavior becomes well-honed. Within three months, the company's retention rate of its sales force tripled.

YOU ARE THERE (BUT NOT REALLY): MIND SCULPTURE

Taking small steps toward your goal will calm your mind and move you forward. But sometimes an activity feels so difficult, so frightening, or so emotionally charged that even a small step feels impossible. In this case, try another kind of small step known as "mind sculpture." Mind sculpture is one of the simplest of kaizen tools and is a way to melt your mental resistance. I often recommend it to people who struggle with sales and public speaking, though it can work with any kind of fear.

Mind sculpture grew out of a psychological technique called "guided imagery." The goal of guided imagery was to help patients improve a physical skill without actually performing the physical act. If a person wanted to improve her speaking ability, for example, she would close her eyes and breathe deeply. When she was in a fully relaxed state, the psychologist would invite her to imagine that she was inside a darkened movie theater, sitting comfortably in front of a blank screen. The patient was then supposed to "see" a movie of herself on the screen, delivering a presentation with panache.

Guided imagery was popular for a while, but its results were lukewarm. It worked, but not nearly as well as people had hoped it would. This general impression was backed up by PET (positron emission tomography) scans, which showed that guided imagery engaged only one part of the brain, the visual cortex. In retrospect, this makes sense. Patients were drawing on their visual imagination, not on the rest of their mental faculties. Why would the rest of the brain bother to get involved?

善

Mind sculpture builds on what psychologists had learned from guided imagery. Mind sculpture is a total sensory experience, albeit an imagined one. Instead of pretending that you see yourself in a movie, you imagine that you are actually performing the activity. You still use your visual cortex. If you are imagining yourself giving a presentation, you look out through your eyes at the audience in front of you, at the painted drywall of the meeting room, and at the white acoustical tiles with their gray pinholes. But you also engage the rest of your brain as you imagine what it's like to move your muscles, to respond emotionally, and to use the rest of your senses: to taste, smell, hear, and touch.

Mind sculpture has been used by athletes to "practice" even when they are sidelined by injuries; when they return to the playing field, they often find that their performance is as strong as ever. Musicians use mind sculpture, too, mentally rehearsing when they are away from their instruments. In one study, a group of people was given a five-finger piano piece to practice for two hours a day. Another group was told to practice—but using only their imaginations. At the end of the study, both groups showed a similar increase in brain activity.

Ian Robertson, a professor of psychology at Trinity College Dublin, the University of Dublin, suggests that mind sculpture works because the brain doesn't distinguish very well between imagination and performance. Imagine yourself performing an activity, and your brain believes it really is doing the work. Repeatedly imagine yourself performing an activity *flawlessly*, and your brain lays down the neural pathways for perfection.[1]

Here's how to use mind sculpture:

1. Choose a skill you want improve or learn. Or choose a situation in which you'd like to feel more comfortable.

2. Decide on an amount of time you can devote to mind sculpture each day. Because you are going to practice an activity that is new or that makes you uneasy, I recommend beginning with no more than one minute. If one minute feels like too much, that's fine. Try 30 seconds. Set a timer, but don't use one with an irritating sound. You want to associate this exercise with pleasure, not with the strident sound of a foghorn or a blare like the one used by the Emergency Broadcast System.

3. Sit in a quiet place. Take a few deep breaths to slow yourself down.

4. Without moving a muscle, imagine that you are immersed in the situation. Examples include:

   a. You are in the conference room of a company, trying to sell your product. Eight key employees of the company are seated around a conference table, their eyes are on you. Imagine yourself making your opening statements. (As you feel more and more comfortable with this exercise, you can imagine making your full pitch.)

b. When you are ready, make the previous exercise a little more challenging. Picture yourself in front of the conference table, with the eight employees present. Imagine that you begin your pitch—and that they respond poorly. Two of them are on their smartphones. One fellow's eyes are half-closed. Maintain your passion, your eye contact, and your articulate focus as you continue your pitch undeterred.

善

111

c. If you tend to respond to your own anxiety unproductively—by using sarcasm, emotionally withdrawing, or talking too fast—mentally place yourself in a tense sales situation. Then imagine yourself responding effectively. Imagine your scalp, your jaw, your shoulders, hands, midsection, and feet all releasing their tension. Feel connected to the other person or people who are with you. Imagine yourself asking the right questions, exploring your customers' needs, and seeking to understand their business with genuine interest. Hear the calm confidence in your voice and the clarity and ease of your words.

5. Practice your mind sculpture each day. Once your daily minute (or 30 seconds) is automatic, effortless, and perhaps even fun, expand the time by a minute or two. How fast you increase your amount

of time is determined by how much you are enjoying the exercise. *Do not increase your time unless the exercise is effortless.* If you start making excuses for not performing your daily mind sculpture, you know that you've asked too much of yourself. Cut your time back. Don't overreach. Assure yourself that a little-by-little kaizen approach will change behaviors for a lifetime; there's no urgency.

改

6. Continue to increase the time you spend on mind sculpture until you achieve one of two possible results.

   a. The first is that you will lay a foundation for change. You'll start to feel so comfortable with mind sculpture that you'll feel ready to try the activity, even if all you manage is one small new step. Maybe you'll want to practice sales with a friend, for example, or make just one sales call a day.

   b. The other possibility is that your brain will "get" the idea and will leap into the new patterns on its own timetable, with no additional conscious effort on your part.

You'll know when mind sculpture has worked when you find yourself in a tough sales situation . . . and you are effortlessly using the words and demeanor you have practiced. Mastering sales will feel like learning to drive a car or to play tennis. The actions that initially feel awkward to you will become automatic, and what at first feels unnatural will become natural.

I saw small thoughts work their magic on a client, Daniel, who is the CEO of a Fortune 50 company. He exults in his job, except for one aspect: public speaking. It's surprising how many great leaders find this task daunting. On the other hand, maybe it's not so surprising. Public speaking is a form of sales, after all. You are trying to "sell" your audience on your company, your idea, or, as in the case of a job interview, yourself. Daniel was like many people in that what he feared, he tried to avoid, so he never acquired the confidence that comes with practice. Of course, he was sometimes forced to hold interviews with stock market analysts or give talks at shareholder meetings, but he found the experience painful and felt that he was acting falsely, not like himself.

Daniel knew he could hire a media trainer to help him, but he had neither the time nor the motivation. I was consulting with him on other matters when he confessed his problem; I told him he could overcome his fear if he would grant me just two minutes a day. Daniel was not convinced the plan would work, but he agreed. He had seen the power of kaizen in the programs we'd instituted at his company and thought it might have some application to his own life.

Because Daniel complained of feeling phony when he delivered talks, we began by focusing not on the style of his delivery but on the content. An awkward style of speaking is often less about personal shyness than it is about *confusion*. Unless a person thoroughly understands why he's speaking and can connect it to his values, he's bound to feel like a fake. Trying to fix Daniel's hesitant delivery without addressing this underlying problem would have been like trying to fix an underbaked cake by slopping on a layer of gooey frosting. Daniel's first small step, therefore, was meant to clear up his haziness about both the corporation mission and his personal one. I invited Daniel to ask himself two questions at the start of each workday:

> *What do we as a company stand for?*
>
> *What about this organization am I proud of today?*

Daniel was busy, but he could manage two questions a day. Note that he wasn't supposed to work on the answers. Once the brain engages a question, you don't need to consciously focus on it. In fact, the process works better if you do the opposite: if you leave the questions to themselves and then engage in other activities. I suspect this is the means by which many people receive ideas they say have come to them from out of the blue. Daniel soon found himself hearing an inner conversation that went like this:

> *We exist for one reason, and that is to provide the best customer service in the world.*
>
> *Integrity and enthusiasm are our highest values.*

These answers reminded Daniel that no matter what the specific topic of his next speech, there were these broader currents that ran beneath.

Daniel's next small step was mind sculpture. His assignment was to spend 30 seconds a day at his desk, sitting back in his chair with his eyes closed as he imagined himself delivering a quarterly update to financial analysts via videoconferencing. He was to put himself so fully into the situation that he could not only hear the words he was using but also the genial and steady vocal tone that represented Daniel at his most confident. I wanted him to see each of analysts on the screen, responding to the sincerity in his voice. He should feel every detail about his body: his spine straight in the chair, his hands making gestures, his jaw relaxed, even feel his tie at his neck and his wool suit scratching slightly against his legs. "Above all," I told Daniel, "think of delivering your message with conviction and enthusiasm, flowing out of the values you share with your company."

When Daniel tried this exercise he was surprised to find himself telling his imaginary audience about times when his employees gave extraordinary service. He also shared a few stories about employees who could have chosen to cut corners to increase profits but decided to maintain quality instead. He had found his voice!

Daniel continued to practice for a few minutes each day. After a few weeks, he felt ready to try more. He continued to imagine his videoconferences, but he added other, more anxiety-provoking, talks to his daily practice. He saw himself giving talks to civic groups and speaking before thousands of people at the annual shareholders' meeting.

After two months of mind sculpture, Daniel noticed that he looked forward to the exercise. He'd developed a taste for public speaking—even if that public speaking was, at this point, mostly still imaginary. Other people who use mind sculpture also experience this enjoyment; when the brain becomes used to an activity, it starts to take pleasure in it. In other words, it becomes a habit.

Daniel began to add extra practice time in the shower and when stuck in traffic. He asked his wife and daughters to serve as a rehearsal audience. As he continued to strengthen his skills, his public speaking became more

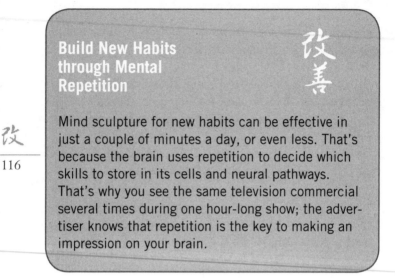

Build New Habits through Mental Repetition

Mind sculpture for new habits can be effective in just a couple of minutes a day, or even less. That's because the brain uses repetition to decide which skills to store in its cells and neural pathways. That's why you see the same television commercial several times during one hour-long show; the advertiser knows that repetition is the key to making an impression on your brain.

effective and one of his favorite parts of the job. This is the magic of mind sculpture; the skill you're practicing becomes so effortless, easy, and routine that you hardly notice the transition from imagination to real life.

CONNECT SALES WITH VALUES

The life of a university fund-raising caller can be pretty dreary. The work takes place in whatever spare facility is available, usually a windowless, bare-walled room with a bunch of mismatched desks and chairs hauled in from neighboring buildings. The callers run down a list of alumni names and phone numbers, asking people to give money to the school. In return for this monotonous work, they score some donations, but they also get hang-ups, angry lectures about how the caller has interrupted family time, and other forms of rejection.

Adam M. Grant, a professor of management at the Wharton School, the University of Pennsylvania, observed the depressing conditions inside a university calling center. He recalls a sign on the wall, posted by a disheartened employee: "Doing a good job here is like wetting your pants in a dark suit. You get a warm feeling, but no one else notices." Within a typical three-month period, the entire staff turned over.

Despite the glum atmosphere, university fund-raising is an essential function. Schools use donations to pay salaries and fund scholarships. A deflated sales staff is less alert and effective—and less likely to bring in the donations that fund the school's good work. Grant wondered if he could energize the callers. He decided against the usual motivating strategies: He didn't suggest that the supervisor make a fiery speech; he rejected the idea of a reward for callers who brought in the most donations; he didn't suggest a swanky remodel of the call center.

Instead, Grant landed on a five-minute solution. He looked up the college kids who had received the scholarships funded by the donations that the callers brought in. He got one of the kids to come in to the call center and make a short, five-minute talk about how he was using the scholarship and what the scholarship meant to him. A month later, the callers who'd heard the student were working much, much harder than before. They spent 142 percent more time on the phone. More important, they were more effective; the amount raised by those callers nearly doubled.

Many corporate studies have proven that people seek meaning and purpose in their work. They want to trace a line between their daily acts and the larger good: When they can make that connection, their work is animated. When they can't make that connection, they burn out, slack off, and eventually quit. As Grant proved, you can help your employees make that connection in one small step.

When you want to enliven your sales staff with the good end results of their work, remember the old writing adage to "show, don't tell." Staff members can be cynical about motivational speeches from their bosses; they suspect that the supervisor is just trying to press more work out of them. It's far more powerful, Grant says, for employees to see the beneficiaries of their work firsthand.

Medtronic, a medical equipment company, has some of its customers attend its annual holiday party. The customers talk about how the company's products have relieved their pain and helped them regain functioning despite chronic illness.[2] The talk is a gift to the staff; it's a way to thank them for their hard work and inspires them to try even harder to deliver a meaningful product to people who need it.

If you can't bring customers into the workplace, look for other ways to make the connection. Grant describes radiologists who worked alone at their computers, never seeing the patients whose scans they were reading. When the doctors were shown photos of the people awaiting their test results, their diagnoses increased in accuracy by 46 percent. Volvo circulates letters from customers who have survived auto accidents thanks to the company's solidly built cars.

Another way to help sales staff connect their work to the civic good is with a vision statement. Do the words "vision statement" make your eyes cross with boredom? Believe me, I know the negative power of an ineffective vision statement. In my career so far, I've worked for three university hospitals. In each case, the vision statement was two or three sentences, far too long for anyone to remember. The hospitals would print the vision statement on the back of the employee badge, in the futile hope that if people looked at it often enough, he or she might recall what it said. I never heard any of those vision statements mentioned by colleagues or attended a meeting in which the vision statement was mentioned. Even when vision statements are more memorable, they don't substitute for the kind of direct testimony that the scholarship recipient gave to the fund-raising callers. And there is no platitude or state-of-the-company speech that can replace the words, tones, and actions leaders use in their daily encounters with staff members.

But when used well, vision statements are powerful tools. They offer employees a guide for their decisions and inspiration to perform the more difficult parts of their jobs. The best vision statements are an embodiment of kaizen. They are simple and short, and they make a connection between the work of the employee and the benefit to the end user.

JetBlue Airways' vision statement is "Safety, Integrity, Caring, Passion, Fun." When a reservations clerk for Jet-Blue is rebooking hundreds of customers who are affected by weather delays, she can remind herself that her mission includes safety and caring. She's helping passengers stay safe by routing them around an icy storm. She's caring for them by offering solutions to their distressing change of plans. What might have been a grueling, brutal day at work becomes a day that, yes, is still hard, but is sparked by meaning and merit. Other vision statements that are gems of clarity include Walt Disney's "To Make People Happy" and Kaiser Hospital's "Best quality, best service, most affordable, best place to work."

One caveat: simple, short vision statements are potent stuff. They work their way under the skin and into the minds of employees, affecting their daily decisions. So take care that these statements express your company's core values. If your mission statement ignores these values, it can backfire.

This is what happened to NASA in the late 1990s. Faced with a shrinking budget, the head of the organization decided to focus the organization's mission on "faster, cheaper, better." The statement worked. People concentrated less on safety and thoroughness, looking instead for ways to cut corners. A landing craft was sent to Mars—and crashed into the surface because of faulty equipment that had not been carefully tested prior to the launch.[3] Later, the *Mars Climate Orbiter* failed because of a mistake in converting English measurements to the metric system. This "minor error" ruined the 125 million-dollar mission. Perhaps a better vision statement would have been "efficient, resourceful, thorough."

When you are thinking of a simple statement for your sales team, beware of saying something like "More sales, bigger sales." Because kaizen vision statements are effective, you may get those results—but at what cost? Will your sales staff make promises to customers that can't be kept? Will they be tempted to game the system and make their sales look bigger than they really are or to steal the accounts of other employees? Be sure your vision statement reflects values that you can uphold.

Kaizen Pathway: Small Steps to Sales

This chapter has explored ways to increase your sales power by simply thinking about sales *differently*. Once you actually make a connection with a customer, there are other small steps you can take to improve sales. These steps are limited only by your imagination, but here are few ideas to get you started:

- *No matter how much money you spend on advertisements, sales occur one customer at a time.* The most effective retail organizations train their staff to view each encounter with a customer as an important investment in future sales. Howard Schultz, the CEO of Starbucks, says, "The only way we can succeed and sustain growth and innovation is linked to the basic elements of one cup of coffee, one customer, and one barista at a time."[4] Look for small ways to "sell" customers on your company with each interaction. Be especially alert for small acts of helpfulness or attention that can cement a relationship.

Singapore Airlines, which is consistently rated in consumer studies as one of the finest airlines in the world, has mastered the small details of customer-employee interaction. As the *Harvard Business Review* remarked, "A passenger may look unwell; another may have no book to read; yet another may have a laptop that has run out of power. Most employees don't pay attention to these small things." But Singapore Airlines employees do.[5]

- *Make sure that the first and last contact your company has with a customer are positive ones.* When Walt Disney first opened the Magic Kingdom at Disneyland, in Anaheim, California, he hired a private company to tend to the parking lot. He soon ended this arrangement, replacing the private company with Disney employees. His reasoning? Members of the parking staff were the first people whom customers saw upon entering Disneyland and the last people they saw upon leaving. Walt Disney wanted to be certain that both impressions would be positive.[6]

- *A great opportunity to increase customer loyalty and sales occurs when your business messes up and you know you have irritated customers.* JetBlue Airways is a dramatic example. In October 2011, JetBlue left thousands of passengers stranded on tarmacs during a severe winter storm. The fiasco made the cover of *BusinessWeek*, and Jet-Blue was the subject of national scorn. Jet-Blue turned this mess into an opportunity to convert the angry customers into loyal ones. JetBlue's staff members personally called every passenger who had been stranded or inconvenienced. Note that this was a personal phone call, not a recording or an e-mail.

  Thanks to their sincere apologies, Jet-Blue rebounded. One formerly disgruntled customer had this to say: "[The JetBlue caller] . . . actually asked me for my opinion of what went wrong and how they could fix it . . . She thanked me for my help and patience and asked me to give the airline a second chance. They got it."[7] This customer is very likely to tell her story to many friends and colleagues. A miserable customer experience was transformed into a marketing success through the very small, but very rare, step of a heartfelt apology.

改

- *After selling, follow through on the relationship.* A dramatic example of follow-through comes from Joe Girard, a car salesman who holds the Guinness World Record for selling 1,425 cars in one year. He said, "When you bought a car from me, you didn't just get a car. You got me." He sent birthday cards to each of his customers, along with monthly postcards that featured different pictures and sayings. When he saw his customers in the dealership's service area, he would greet them and make sure they were being taken care of. If a service bill was only 10 or 15 dollars, he would wait for his customer to ask, "How much do I owe you?" Girard would respond, "Nothing. I love you. Just come back." The results spoke for themselves. Girard was so busy that when customers wanted to buy their next car, they had to make appointments first![8]

As you think about steps you can take to improve your interaction with customers, you can always rely on your own inner knowledge. Ask yourself, "What's one small way I can improve sales?" Give the question a few days to simmer, and let your mind cook up a response that's individually made for you and the product or service that you sell.

Chapter Seven

REDUCE HEALTH-CARE EXPENSES

You may not enjoy having to rouse your employees to improve their health habits, but kaizen makes things simple and even pleasant.

A few decades ago, no one would have dreamed that managers could or should feel responsible for changing their employees' health habits. Yet as health care has become a significant cost for organizations, that's what has happened. If staff members get healthy, the organization saves money.

One way corporations encourage their employees to do better is through incentives:

they offer money to people who can demonstrate improved health behaviors. Another method is to apply social pressure, with departments competing against one another to see which can lose the most weight. Even when these external motivators work, employees tend to relapse into their old behaviors when the program is over and the reward or the pressure is removed.

As employers are discovering, any attempt to change health behaviors encounters serious resistance. When General Motors removed cigarette-vending machines from their factories, a company physician told me, employees began selling cigarettes to their colleagues out of the trunks of their cars. You can try lunch-and-learn lectures or a big-ticket wellness program, but you may find that the employees who eagerly sign on are the lean, fit ones who are already motivated to take care of themselves. They don't really need the program. Meanwhile, the staff members who really could benefit from health advice will retreat behind their office doors or quietly slide off for cups of coffee whenever it's time to participate in a wellness event.

Don't be too hard on these folks. Losing weight, eating better, and beginning an exercise program are some of the toughest changes a person can make. You can possess a blistering self-discipline in your business life but still struggle when it's time to resist the mashed potatoes.

Why are health changes so hard for people? For any number of reasons, including these:

- They are busy.
- They are tired.
- They don't have enough support.

- Their partners sabotage their efforts.

- They have developed bad habits or behaviors that are etched into their psyches and are deeply comforting. Such habits include overeating or spending most of their free time wrapped in a cozy blanket on the couch.

Each of these obstacles to change is important, but underlying them all is *fear*. Recall a premise of kaizen: *Change is frightening*. Remember, too, the physiology of change. At the first whiff of fear, the amygdala (the body's alarm mechanism, tucked away in the midbrain) sets off a cascade of reactions that make it more likely that a person will resist change. This reaction to fear is why it's so hard to stop eating French fries or begin an exercise program—even if you believe it will be a positive change if you do, and even if you know that your health will suffer if you don't. Your thinking brain says, "Today, let's go for a walk instead of eating a muffin from the snack cart." But this reasonable suggestion is drowned out by the amygdala, which is shrieking, "I sense change! Danger! Danger!"

In the self-help literature, a popular approach to this dilemma is to ask people to face down their fears. In this approach, you dig up your psyche, root out the traumas or garden-variety disappointments, and hold them up to the light. Once you have candidly examined your fears, the argument states, you should be free to make your changes without impediment. This works . . . but only sometimes.

Don't get me wrong; I'm a psychologist, and I've seen how this kind of deep analysis can be lifesaving. But if you're a manager, unearthing your staff's personal problems is not your territory. Even if you wanted to go there, it wouldn't be appropriate for you to do so. But that's okay. When it comes to making health changes, deep psychological work just isn't necessary for everyone. Even in my private consulting business—where it would be more than appropriate for me to "go deep" with clients—I sometimes work with people who have been sent to me by their doctors with orders to lose weight or start exercising, stat. Their health is at immediate risk. There isn't time for a complete psychological upheaval before making that change happen. And some clients have the luxury of more time to make a change, but they are so unaware of their fears and blocks that they can't easily get at them.

This is where kaizen is remarkably, even shockingly, useful. Think of it as a mellow detour around a supersensitive nervous system. By taking very—*very*—small steps, people can move so softly and quietly toward change that their fears are never aroused. The amygdala never goes into that self-sabotaging alert mode, and before they are even aware of what they are doing, they've built a positive new set of habits. This is, truly, change without stress.

How do you encourage employees to take kaizen steps? You can't, not until you are convinced that kaizen for health really works. So read on. In the pages to come, I'll describe how two people used kaizen to change their health habits, even after other approaches—including willpower, self-control, and a doctor's urgent orders—failed. You'll also see scientific evidence for small steps, along with suggestions for ways that employees can apply kaizen to health goals.

Once you are convinced of the power and charm of kaizen for health, you can spread the word to your employees. Throughout this chapter, I'll talk about ways you can encourage them to take kaizen steps, without seeming pushy or causing defensiveness.

PORTION CONTROL AND STRESS MANAGEMENT: ROGER'S STORY

Roger, a partner in a law firm, has never had a weight problem. When he came to see me, however, his diet was far from ideal. As one of the firm's most visible and successful rainmakers, Roger went to business dinners to eat several nights a week. He always pledged to choose his meals wisely, but once he took a look at the menu he was a goner. He ate enormous, rich meals and washed down all the sugar and saturated fat with at least two cocktails. His physician, alarmed by Roger's soaring blood pressure, cholesterol, and triglycerides, spoke to him sternly, explaining that Roger was at high risk for a coronary.

Roger heard the message. But this understanding didn't translate into a change in his eating patterns. After his wife pleaded with him to "get some help," Roger came to see me.

I've mentioned that it's not necessary to wander down the darkest corridors of your psyche to use kaizen steps. That's true. When Roger came for his first visit, however, he was at the ready with two theories about why it was so hard for him to control his eating. As you'll see, we used these theories to design his kaizen steps—but I think you'll also grasp that small steps could have been useful for him even without this initial psychological work.

Roger's first theory about the cause of his overeating was that when he was a child, his parents had always urged him to clean his plate. A good boy, Roger did as he was told. Now, decades later, he still felt guilty if he didn't polish off every last crumb. Roger's second theory was that food and drinks were his consolation prizes for working at a career that he'd come to find grueling and barren of meaning. When he could eat and drink well, he was getting pleasure that he did not receive from his work life.

These theories sounded on the mark to me. When Roger lamented that he felt no strong motivation to change, not even after his doctor had warned him about the grave consequences of continuing his habits, we decided to try a kaizen approach. We would sneak up on the change; that way, Roger wouldn't even have the chance to reject it.

I decided to target the "clean your plate" compulsion first because Roger wasn't just eating fatty food, he was eating *heaps* of fatty food. And although Roger somehow managed to remain slim, I'll point out here that portion control is often a good place to start when you are trying to lose weight. Study after study shows that the main factor in weight loss and weight maintenance isn't switching the kind of food you eat; it's learning to eat less of it.

I asked Roger to think of a small, trivial-seeming step that would help him leave some food on his plate. Roger responded by suggesting, "I should just eat less." But that was too big a goal and way too vague—plus, he'd told himself to eat less in the past, and it had never worked.

"Think smaller," I said.

Roger wondered if maybe he should try to leave half the food on his plate.

"You're getting the idea," I said. "That's a more specific step, but it's still too big."

Roger thought and said, "What if I throw out the last bite?"

That was a small step, indeed. I made one tweak: I asked Roger to throw out the *first* bite. When you're at the end of a good meal, throwing out the last bite is just too hard, especially if you're reading from a childhood script that says, "Leaving food on your plate is immoral." Roger realized that it would be odd-looking if he made a big show of throwing away the first bite of food at a business dinner, so we agreed that he would pull a bite's worth of food to the side of his plate and discreetly spoil it with pepper or a condiment he found distasteful.

By itself, this step was not going to lower Roger's blood pressure, cholesterol, or triglycerides. But the point of this tiny step was to detour past Roger's mental alarm system and lay down a system for change. You'll know you've found the perfect small step when it is so effortless that you are absolutely certain you can do it.

Roger, in fact, was able to spoil his first bite without any resistance at all. He spent a month developing this habit, and was surprised at how much gratification he derived from this tiny success. The next month, Roger spoiled the first two bites of his restaurant meals. Then he moved up to spoiling three bites' worth of food. By the fourth month, Roger reported that when he was done eating, there was often additional food on his plate that he left behind. He wasn't sure how this change had happened; it just did. His brain had created a new neural pathway—a new habit—of not eating everything on his plate.

As Roger continued to reduce his portion sizes, we turned to his alcohol consumption. Let me be clear: Roger was not suffering from an alcohol addiction. (Although kaizen can be useful to help people kick their drinking, smoking, or other addictions, I suggest enlisting professional help as well.) But he did have a bad habit of knocking back those two cocktails at every business dinner, and the cocktails had a ripple effect. The first ripple was that the alcohol inhibited his self-control. When Roger drank, his doctor's warnings seemed to recede, and he cared less about eating well. The second ripple affected Roger's sleep. Alcohol can make it easier to drift off to sleep at the beginning of the night, but that sleep tends to be thin and unrefreshing. Having a drink close to bedtime also leads to frequent night wakings and less total sleep over the course of a night.

Roger reported that he drank his cocktails almost unconsciously, hardly noticing their flavor as he sent them down the hatch. I suggested this kaizen step: for each sip of alcohol he took, Roger was to take two sips of water. Notice that I did not ask him to resolve to drink less alcohol. That would have been too hard at the start. But this step helped him slow down and become more mindful as he drank. It also lessened the effects of the alcohol.

Finally, we took on Roger's view that food was his well-deserved reward for concluding a tiresome, unfulfilling day. Instead of telling Roger to rush out and make a career change, I wanted him to try two kaizen techniques to make his current work more satisfying. Research suggests that physical health and productivity are enhanced by honoring the body's ultradian cycles, which occur in periods of about 90 to 120 minutes. The body can sustain its focus and energy for one of those cycles, but then it runs out of zip. It begins a kind of protest march in the form of physical symptoms such as fatigue, yawning, irritability, hunger, or restlessness. These signs can look like chronic unhappiness, but what they are really trying to tell is you that your body is simply craving a recovery period. According to a study reported in the *Harvard Business Review*, a short rest—between three and five minutes—can be enough to recharge the brain for another ultradian cycle. (In the study, the short breaks usually involved a distracting activity. Light exercise and reading the newspaper were popular choices.)[1] If you listen to these cycles, you'll be rewarded with greater health, productivity, and pleasure.

Roger had approached his workdays like a man walking into a strong wind; he hunched over and powered through until he reached the end, when he was so ready for some gratification that he ate anything and everything that looked good. I suspect that Roger thought that this pattern of deprivation and reward was a sign of a virtuous life. But he recognized that something wasn't working, so he agreed that every 90 minutes at work he'd take a short, five-minute break. He thought he would enjoy reading the sports page or just sitting quietly and breathing in a deep, relaxed fashion. Roger had been keeping business and pleasure divided into two separate compartments; by mixing some enjoyable activities into his work day, we hoped he would feel less need to escape into bingeing at night.

I also used a kaizen question designed to help Roger locate the meaning in his work. I gave him an index card, on which he wrote these words: *How am I being of service to my clients, my staff, or my family today?*

Roger was to read the card at least twice a day—and he was specifically *not* supposed to work very hard to find an answer. Remember that the mind has a special attraction to small questions. You don't have to actively brainstorm a list of answers or spend time journaling about your ideas. All you have to do is ask the question of yourself and let your cerebral cortex get to work. Within about three weeks, Roger began to "hear" answers that his mind had produced:

> *I'm helping a client solve a problem.*
>
> *I'm providing employment for assistants, paralegals, law librarians, and other staff members.*
>
> *I'm bringing resources to my family.*

Do these answers sound unspectacular? Predictable? I certainly could have offered Roger this wisdom during our first session, saying something like, "You do useful and productive work, so stop feeling so glum!" But those words would have evaporated into meaninglessness. When Roger discovered—on his own—how his work served others, the answers took on a truthfulness and power.

After less than six months, Roger was eating and drinking much less. His stress levels improved, too. What was Roger's favorite part of the change process? That he never had to undertake any task that lasted longer than five minutes.

2. To lose two pounds over the course of a year—without changing what you eat—drink four or more cups of water per day. Place a bottle of water at your desk, by your bathroom mirror, or in your car, to remind you to drink.

3. People who overindulge in sweets often eat very quickly, without really enjoying their food. Try to put down your fork, spoon, or candy bar between each bite. The slower you eat, the sooner you'll feel satisfied.

4. One of the strongest determinants of fullness is purely psychological: it's whether you finish eating everything that's given to you. To feel full with less food, put your meal on a smaller plate.

5. Ask a waiter to box up half your meal *before* bringing it the table.

6. Take a plastic bag to restaurants. When the bread arrives, place it in the bag and put it out of sight.

7. In fast-food restaurants, order the children's meal. The size is smaller. And you get a toy.

8. If you tend to eat when you are upset, experiment with other ways of self-comforting. When you feel tense or sad, try to:

   a. Drink lots of water.

   b. Journal.

   c. Call a friend.

   d. Exercise for a minute or two.

   e. Breathe slowly.

SMALL STEPS FOR BETTER EATING

Very small changes can leverage a significant effect on health. Consider these kaizen findings about weight loss and health:

- A 10 percent decrease in cholesterol levels can result in a 30 percent reduction in the incidence of coronary artery disease.

- Losing one pound a year for four years and keeping it off can reduce one's risk of hypertension by 25 percent.

135

Other changes work by accumulation. They may be small in themselves, but over the course of time they can add up to a mighty transformation. Although no one likes to be preached to or nagged at—especially when it comes to eating habits—you can try giving a super-short, five-minute talk on kaizen. Say something like, "If this is a time for you to make big changes, go for it! But if big changes don't seem to work for you, try kaizen." You can talk about the evidence or, if it's applicable, your own experience with kaizen health. Suggest these small steps toward the end of the talk, or post them in the break room. And encourage employees to come up with their own kaizen methods for eating better. Here are 10 highly doable suggestions that you can share with your employees:

1. If you can eliminate a habitual morning doughnut, bagel, or muffin and replace it with cereal or toast, you can lose 10 or 15 pounds in a year.

9. Try mind sculpture to teach your brain new habits. For five seconds every day, picture yourself in a restaurant:

   a. Talking to a dinner companion.

   b. Eating slowly.

   c. Drinking water.

   d. Leaving some food on your plate.

   Each week, add an additional five seconds to this exercise. Eventually, and without making a conscious effort, you will find yourself reducing your portion sizes.

10. Go to bed a minute earlier every night for a week. Use that minute to practice slow, deep breathing. Or you can read something you find pleasurable. Sleep deprivation triggers two hormones, leptin and ghrelin, which affect carbohydrate cravings. The next week, go to bed two minutes earlier. Continue the pattern until you no longer feel sleepy when arising in the morning.

If you're feeling motivated, you can try another small intervention: e-mail reminders. One study divided 787 office workers into two groups. The first group received weekly e-mails and mid-week reminders about one of three behaviors of the group members' choosing. These reminders were to:

1. Increase physical activity.

2. Increase fruit and vegetable intake.

3. Lower intake of sugar and saturated fats.

The reminders were very brief and contained a small suggestion, such as go for a walk during a coffee break, order a salad with chicken for lunch, and avoid the sweets in the break room. The second group received no intervention.

At the end of the 16-week experiment, the first group had increased their exercise by an average of an hour each week, reduced saturated fats by more than a gram per day, or increased fruit and vegetable consumption by an average of one-third of a cup daily. The second group showed no changes in their health behaviors.[2]

Try asking your employees if they'd like to receive weekly or mid-week health reminders. Keep those reminders light and encouraging . . . and include a small suggestion.

EXERCISING, STEP BY STEP: AMY'S STORY

Amy started gaining weight while working toward her master of business administration (MBA). By the time she graduated, she thought of herself as fat. Then she entered the workforce and continued to gain four or five pounds each year. "I don't understand," Amy said, "how I can be so driven in my career but lack willpower and self-control when it comes to my weight." In fact, her 11-hour workdays were part of the problem. She had joined a gym, but she was too busy and tired to use it, even on the weekends.

Amy's annual physical revealed that she had high cholesterol and that, given her family history, she was at risk for diabetes. Amy was referred to me by her doctor, but she was hesitant that I was just going to tell her what she already knew: to exercise more and eat less.

Fortunately for Amy and me, she had learned about kaizen in business school. Like most other people, she hadn't considered using it outside of production; she certainly hadn't imagined applying kaizen to her weight problems. But when I showed her evidence that even small changes can lead to significant health improvement, she was on board.

Most people can intuit which health habit is likely to be a catalyst that links to further positive change. Amy felt strongly that if she could begin exercising again, she'd feel better and be more likely to eat well. Yet she still faced her ongoing problem: How could she exercise when she was so fatigued?

We agreed on one minute of exercise each day. Each morning, as she watched the morning financial news, Amy would move in place in front of the television. A week later, Amy was proud of her modest but consistent success. She liked this feeling of achievement so much that she decided not to risk failure. For one more month, Amy decided, she'd do her one minute a day—and nothing more. On several days, however, she found herself doing two minutes. One day she started marching in place during the news and kept going until the program was over.

"I didn't really notice that I was still marching," she said. Forgetting to stop your new, positive habit is a classic sign that kaizen is working its stuff.

It was still important to proceed slowly. The next month, Amy added a different "workout" to her routine: while on the phone, she would stand up or pace around the room instead of sitting at her desk. The month after that, she went up one flight of stairs, adding one step—not one flight—each day. One little step isn't going to improve anybody's blood sugar all by itself, but add one step each day for six months and you have real cardiovascular activity.

This is what happened to Amy. She was marching during the morning news, pacing on her phone calls, and climbing several flights of stairs each day. She began to enjoy the game of looking for small ways to increase her movement. Once she called me from the airport, laughing, to say that she wished the other passengers knew about kaizen. If they did, Amy told me, they wouldn't stand in place on the escalator!

As Amy predicted, she began to eat less without a whole lot of effort. (Notice that she stopped talking in terms of "willpower" and "self-control," which are poor defenses against an amygdala that's on high alert.) She lost the weight and, by literally taking small steps, gained a life-long habit of exercise.

ONE-MINUTE EXERCISE MIRACLES

It's not actually a miracle when someone begins an exercise plan and sticks to it, but often it feels like one. When people think of themselves as exercise failures, kaizen offers an easier path to success.

There is strong evidence that even very small amounts of exercise translate into health benefits. For example, a study reported in the *Journal of Clinical Nutrition* found that short bouts of exercise, just three minutes each, for a total of 30 minutes a day, lowered several measures of cardiac risk as effectively as one continuous 30-minute

Kaizen
by Example

If you can't imagine yourself talking to employees about health behaviors, don't worry. Try modeling those behaviors instead:

- When you are walking with an employee to another department, take the stairs instead of the escalator.
- If you need to work on portion control, let employees see you put aside the first bite of your lunch.
- Take rest breaks where you can be seen by the staff.
- Put healthy snacks on top of your desk.
- Take a more direct approach to modeling health habits by putting a chart on your wall that reflects how many steps you've climbed that day.

If an employee asks you a question like, "Why are you putting aside that bite of food?" or "Do you really think that walking up one flight of stairs can make a difference?" you have a natural opener to describe kaizen in greater detail.

141

session. That's good news for all of us, because it's easier to convince employees to move for three minutes than for 30 minutes.

But when even three minutes of motion is too much, here's a study for you: A Mayo Clinic experiment used "data-logging underwear"—essentially a set of wearable pedometers—to compare two groups of nonexercisers: one group was overweight and one group was lean. Both groups were controlled for metabolic rates. Much like Amy, the lean group was more active in small ways during the day. The lean group walked up escalators, took the stairs instead of the elevator if they were going just a few floors up, paced across their office while talking on the phone, and parked farther away in the parking lot. This difference in activity led to an expenditure of 350 calories extra each day, and over the course of a year, a 30- to 40-pound difference in weight.

For a different take on exercise, consider this study from King County in Washington state: a 1999 study of more than 800 residents showed dramatic health benefits among those who gardened or walked for just an hour a week. This added up to 400 or 500 calories burned and a 70 percent lower risk of sudden cardiac death.

When you need to encourage employees to exercise, deliver this optimistic message: every calorie burned is an accomplishment. Instead of trying to blast off 750 calories in an hour, which is hard for most nonathletes, apply the philosophy of "continual improvement" to your exercise routine. That is, look for very small ways to burn an additional couple of calories, increase your aerobic capacity, or accomplish other health benefits. Here are some suggestions:

1. Move in place for one minute each day, perhaps while watching television or listening to music. Add one minute each week.

2. If you work in a high-rise, go up one flight of stairs on the first day. Each day, add a single stair step.

3. Stand and/or pace when you are on the phone or thinking through a problem.

4. Do five pushups or sit-ups a day. Each week, add one more.

5. Even if your luggage has wheels, pick it up and carry it part of the time while you are traveling.

6. Walk up or down escalators.

7. At work or at shopping centers, park as far from the entrance as you can and walk the rest of the way in.

8. When you are working, take a break every 90 minutes. Spend about five minutes doing stretches or take a stroll through the office. Because the brain works on 90-minute cycles, you not only burn calories, you give your brain the rest it craves and you improve its performance.

9. In very large meetings or conferences, sit toward the back of the room. Every now and then, move to the back wall and do some unobtrusive stretches or pace back and forth. (You'll look like you are thinking.)

10. Try mind sculpture. For five seconds each day, imagine that you are running, playing tennis, or lifting weights. Imagine you are looking through your eyes as you perform the activity; notice how the activity feels in your muscles. You might not burn any calories during mind sculpture, but if you add five more seconds each week, you will eventually notice that you are moving more often in real life.

改

Kaizen should be easy. Ask employees to choose a step that they are sure they can do. This step should feel automatic and effortless before they add on it. And no one needs to feel as if they were born to be inactive. If your employees feel discouraged, tell them to remember their childhoods, a time when they were always eager to play and to move. Sitting down to meals was boring. They can recover this natural joy in moving their bodies—but it is best to get there via small steps.

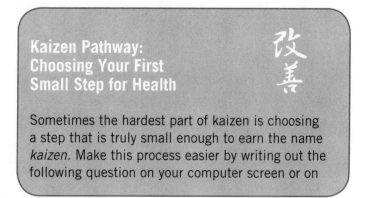

Kaizen Pathway: Choosing Your First Small Step for Health

Sometimes the hardest part of kaizen is choosing a step that is truly small enough to earn the name *kaizen*. Make this process easier by writing out the following question on your computer screen or on a piece of paper: *What is the smallest step you could take toward improvement?*

If you're like most people, your answer will be too ambitious or too vague. You'll say something like, "I should exercise more" or—going off the topic of health and wellness—"I should get a promotion and a raise to go with it." These answers are noble, but they will trigger your amygdala's fear of change. The alarm bells will call out in distress, your cerebral cortex will go dark, and you'll end up where you began.

This is why it's wise to ask yourself this question over and over. Your brain will play with the question and actually enjoy the game. So look down at your question and ask yourself again: *What is the smallest step you can take toward improvement?*

On the second try, you will probably come up with a smaller step. But it may still not be kaizen. Even steps such as "walk during my lunch break" or "ask for a promotion" are too big. So give it one more try: *What's the smallest step you can take toward improvement?*

At this point, you're forced to get more creative. How about "walk outside and eat my lunch in the park?" or "imagine myself asking for a promotion"? Now *that's* kaizen! Once you take that first step, you'll learn what success feels like. Better yet, you'll develop a taste for it. Continue with that step until one of two things happen: either you find yourself improving—without even realizing it—or the step becomes so automatic and effortless that you are eager for more.

改

Chapter Eight

WHEN SMALL STEPS ARE TOO HARD: WHAT TO DO

When even small steps are too hard, it's a sign that your fears are waking up. Here are five ways to quiet those fears and move down the kaizen path to your goal.

Small steps work. But if you're heading toward a major change, you may feel like some of my clients, the ones who say, "Even small steps make me panic!" Resistance in any form—fear, panic, resignation, boredom—is a sign that fears are waking up. There are as many reasons to fear change as there are people on the planet. But there are five very common obstacles that nearly everyone has encountered. They cause all kinds of resistance and send us running for the hills. They make us want to give up on our most cherished hopes. The five obstacles are:

1. An overwhelming crisis

2. Fear and anxiety

3. A harsh, critical inner voice

4. Isolation

5. Looking for answers in the wrong place

These obstacles can pop up no matter what kind of change you're seeking. When you encounter them, it's time to stop, reevaluate, slow down . . . and then break the steps for change down into such tiny pieces that resistance gently dissolves. No forcing, no fighting, no agonized self-recrimination. I'll describe the kinds of small steps that tend to be especially useful in response to each obstacle and will show you how to avoid the cascade of neurochemical reactions that make change so difficult. If your steps are small enough, you'll stay on the path to improvement, and your organization will experience the benefits of incremental but steadily accumulating change.

OBSTACLE 1:
AN OVERWHELMING CRISIS

When you're in a business crisis, the pressures can be crushing. Under these circumstances, drastic steps are particularly alluring. You may want to do *anything* to make the fears, the angry self-criticism, and other negatives, such as harassment from your supervisors or shareholders, go away. This feeling of urgency can occur, no matter whether the crisis was caused by your own actions or was the result of unforeseeable circumstances. Either way, you're in a vise.

If you are able to take large, rational steps to solve your crisis, by all means do so.

149

But be careful. When you desperately want relief, you can leave yourself vulnerable to bad decisions. For example, small-business owners who are facing bankruptcy have been known to sell their best assets at fire-sale prices just to get the payments off their conscience. Not-for-profits that are in need of cash can be too eager to accept a private citizen's donation, even if it has some ugly strings attached. Companies with a major public-relations disaster on their hands may decide that the best way to handle the crisis is to vigorously deny the problem and defend themselves; this is a step that almost always makes the problem worse.

When there is so much fear at play, small steps are a lifeline. I'm thinking here of Gina, who owned a small biotech start up. The company had begun with plenty of funding, but a combination of overspending and tight credit meant that it had landed in trouble. If it continued on its current path, investors would start to pull out. Gina was humiliated by what she saw as her own role in mismanaging the company's money. She hadn't done anything illegal or unethical, but, looking back with the benefit of hindsight, she felt that she had spent too much on what now seemed like luxuries, such as high-end furniture for the offices and lavish gifts for her best customers.

Gina had used kaizen to solve other problems at work, but in her current overwhelmed state she couldn't get motivated to try small steps to ease her crisis. She would come up with ideas for saving a thousand dollars here or a few hundred dollars there, but she couldn't follow through. At our first session together, I suggested she take the small steps and *shrink* them, making them into micro-steps.

I started by asking Gina if she, personally, could save one dollar for her business each day. This was a smaller step than Gina had imagined. One dollar a day wouldn't erase the company's debt, not even if it had 50 years to repay its loans—but to my surprise, Gina received my suggestion thoughtfully. She was a scientist, she explained, and she understood that with this step she could be building a new system of behavior.

Gina's first small money-saving step was to order water instead of soda or coffee when she went out to lunch during the week. The following week, she saved 50 cents more each day by reading the newspaper online instead buying a newsstand copy. (This was half of her dollar goal, but that was okay with me, because the amount of savings was less important than taking some kind of action.) Remember, small steps train the brain; you'll make the big leaps once you have programmed your thinking for the new behaviors you desire.

By the fifth week, Gina eagerly volunteered multiple ways she was saving money:

- Brown-bagging lunch

- Organizing her desk and finding small supplies—pens, staples, and so on—that she had thought were lost

- Photocopying documents on both sides of the paper

She reported that saving money, once difficult for her, had become an absorbing pastime. This was another sign that a fundamental change was underway. Not surprisingly, Gina started mulling over for some larger changes as well. Within a few more weeks, Gina had renegotiated deals with two of her suppliers. She had also talked to another start-up firm about sharing her office space, which would cut her rent in half. When she landed a new customer, she sent the company a handwritten note instead of a gift.

About a year later, Gina sent me a postcard. Her company was on much more solid footing. "I'm writing you a postcard," she added at the end, "because it's less expensive than a letter."

In a crisis it can be hard to see the utility of small steps. If you owe your vendors hundreds of thousands—or millions—of dollars, saving money by cutting back on soda seems abjectly ridiculous. Why bother? I'll tell you why. Small steps create neural pathways in your brain, laying down tracks that detour around all your old problems—the fears, the mental blocks—and create new, better habits that allow you to change the way your company functions. Small steps also satisfy your amygdala's desire for action, so you feel calmer. This is true for any kind of corporate crisis, not just a financial one. You'll feel a greater mastery of your situation, enough that you are able to pause, look around, and make decisions from a position of self-control, not panic.

OBSTACLE 2: FEAR AND ANXIETY

Fear and anxiety are normal responses to change. Unfortunately, they rob you of clearheaded thinking. If fear makes you feel desperate, you might also try to erase your pain by abandoning your attempts at change and returning to the status quo.

Action dispels fear. If you can take small steps toward making your change, you'll feel calmer. But when your anxiety is running feverishly high, try some small steps that are precisely targeted toward decreasing it. My favorite small step for anxiety is based on a biological fact: it's impossible to be relaxed—and to achieve the creativity that occurs with relaxation—when you are breathing rapidly. So I want you to take 10 slow, deep breaths, right now. Try the four-eight-four technique:

- Breathe in to a count of four.
- Hold to a count of eight.
- Breathe out to a count of four.

Do the four-eight-four technique 10 times whenever:

- You sit down at your desk to take stock of the problem that's bothering you, the one you want to change.
- Your supervisor calls and demands to know what you are doing to meet your goals.
- You feel the urge to quit.
- You can't sleep.
- You start to feel anxious for any reason.

Maybe you are thinking: *How can a few deep breaths end my anxiety, when my feelings are based on real deadlines and real trouble?* They won't. Deep breathing is just one small step. Don't expect too much from it, especially in the first few days of practice. But after a week goes by, don't be surprised if you enjoy having some control over your physical response to fear. You might even want to try other steps to alleviate fear, such as:

- For five seconds, identify a tense muscle and imagine that it is melting, like a pool of hot butter.
- Three or four times a day, ask yourself, *What is one thing that I'm grateful for at this moment?*
- Notice whether your shoulders are hovering up around your ears. If they are, bring your shoulders down to their normal position.
- Stand up straight.

No matter whether you have serious problems or just a lot of free-floating change anxiety, taking small steps toward relaxation will help you feel more hope and possibility. Maybe just a glimmer, but sometimes that's all you need to take you down the path toward your goals. When you are ready—and give yourself plenty of time to feel ready—draw the first step of your own map.

OBSTACLE 3:
A HARSH, CRITICAL INNER VOICE

Read the following statements:

I'm an idiot!

Why is everything so much harder for me than it is for everyone else?

If I weren't so stupid, I wouldn't have to use small steps.

改

154

Do they sound familiar? When kaizen seems hard, it's often because a harsh, critical inner voice is blocking the way. Ironically, many people believe a loop of punishing self-talk is brutal but necessary. They think it's like having a tough-talking coach in their head who spurs them on to success. These people worry that if they speak to themselves with kindness, they will become lazy and complacent. This is untrue. Negative thoughts do have power—but it's the power to slow you down, trip you up, and thwart your best intentions. Life's truly successful people —the ones who create, invent, progress, and lead—speak to themselves more encouragingly. They enjoy themselves more, too.

You need to get this overly critical voice out of your head, but here's the catch: You cannot get a harsh and angry voice to leave by talking to it in a harsh and angry voice. You have to develop some new moves.

Start by knowing this: The critical voice was programmed into your midbrain a long time ago. It may be the voice of a parent or a teacher, or it may be an inner voice you developed as a way of coping with life's problems before you knew any other way of handling them. No matter what the origin of this voice, it's now as automatic as the language you speak. To rescript your inner voice, you'll need to call on your thinking brain, the cerebral cortex. Unlike the reactive, primitive midbrain, the cerebral cortex knows how to nurture and instruct. It looks for ways to help rather than to rebuke.

The good news is that the cortex is a creature of habit. Advertisers pay to air the same commercial three or four times during the same television program because they know psychology: to create a new behavior, such as buying a certain product, repetition is key. Use this knowledge to your advantage.

Three or four times a day, note what you're doing and then pause. Imagine the person you like best on the whole planet. Imagine that person is engaged in the same behavior and getting the very same result you're getting. What words of praise, suggestion, or instruction would you speak to that person? What tone of voice would you use? Almost certainly the words will be more heartening than what your inner voice says to *you*. Now turn those very same words toward yourself. If possible, say them out loud. Within a month, your cortex will accept the new behavior of gentler, more encouraging self-talk and it will become automatic. At this point, you can resume kaizen steps toward your original goal.

OBSTACLE 4: ISOLATION

What do you do when you've got a problem? Do you pull up the drawbridge, stock the moat with crocodiles, and tend to the problem in the safety of your own castle?

Independence may be a virtue, but isolation is a killer. The myth of self-reliance is just that: a myth. Successful people may look as if they climbed to the top on the basis of their talents and their can-do spirit—and those qualities certainly help. But the successful people also rely on networks and communities to help them through the tough times. If you respond to business problems by building walls around yourself or your staff, you are setting yourself up for depression and despair. You also deprive yourself of resources for addressing the issue.

Small steps can work even if you're all on your own. But small steps are much more effective when you let them move you toward the people who can provide concrete assistance or the kind of personal support that will reduce your fears and unleash your productivity.

The problem is that asking for help doesn't come naturally to many of us. You can, however, become more comfortable reaching out to others and asking for cooperation or assistance. Twice a day, ask yourself these small questions:

> *Who could I ask for help?*
>
> *What kind of help could I ask for?*

Within a week or so, answers will bubble to the surface. One couple I know ran a small business and fell into serious straits. The wife had developed leukemia and their time and financial resources were being drained by the disease. They needed a retail sales manager who could step in to run the business while they were focused on medical treatments, and they needed a money strategy that kept their personal expenses separate from their business. These were good, responsible, hardworking business owners. Neither was accustomed to leaning on anyone else. Yet it was clear that they needed help.

Twice a day, they asked each other, out loud: "Who could you ask for help? What kind of help would you ask for?" For the first three days, they each came up with the same answer: "I don't know." But by the fourth day, they began to consider—to their great surprise—the possibility of asking members of their professional alliances, their siblings, the hospital, and debt-relief agencies for assistance. It relieved their minds to discover that external resources did, in fact, exist.

善

157

Mind Sculpture: Asking for Help

改善

The kaizen technique of mind sculpture—fully imagining a difficult task by drawing on all your senses—can help you get more comfortable asking for assistance. Here's how to do it:

- *Close your eyes and imagine your potential benefactor standing before you.* Imagine every aspect of the situation: What does he or she look like? What kind of room are you in? Can you feel the air-conditioning or smell the microwave popcorn drifting from somewhere down the hall?
- *Now imagine yourself asking for help.* What words do you use? What is your tone of voice? What clothes are you wearing?

改

> Imagine yourself feeling calm, with your muscles relaxed and your posture erect.
> - *Finally, imagine the answer.* How do you respond if the answer is "No"? Or "Yes"?
> - *If this exercise is difficult for you, practice it just three, four, or five seconds a day.* As it becomes less painful, increase the amount of time by a few seconds, and bump up your practice sessions to twice daily. Continue to increase the time in small increments until you are comfortable with this mind sculpture. At this point, you are ready to ask a real live person for assistance.

They were still shy about actually asking for help, however. I assigned them the small step of mind sculpture. Instead of picking up the phone and having a conversation that felt embarrassing, they spent a few seconds each day just imagining themselves making their request. Within a few days, they felt ready to begin letting others help. They were startled to find that their colleagues and neighbors had been hoping for an opportunity to lend a hand.

OBSTACLE 5: LOOKING FOR ANSWERS IN THE WRONG PLACE

In 2010, David H. Freedman wrote an article for *Discover*, "Why Scientific Studies Are So Often Wrong: The Streetlight Effect."[1] It's based on the old story of the man who is crawling around underneath a streetlight. A policeman comes up to the man and asks him what he is doing.

"I'm looking for my keys," the man replies.

And then he points down the street and says, "I dropped them over there."

The officer is puzzled. "If you dropped them over there, why are you looking for them here?"

The man believes the answer is obvious. "Because the light is better here," he says.

Freedman points out that we can all be like the man in the story; we all tend to look for answers in the places where the looking is easiest. I'd add that when our goals feel too difficult to reach, we try to distract ourselves by solutions where we are, relatively, more comfortable. Sometimes we even forget what our real goal is.

An example is Sarah, a working artist and beloved faculty member at her state's university. When she sought therapeutic help, it was to discuss her strategies regarding a new job offer in a distant city. Her concern was real. The job offer involved higher status and pay; unfortunately, it would take her away from her friends and family. She felt torn, and I could understand why. But as we began to talk, a fuller story developed: Her marriage had recently fallen apart. She had been struggling with feelings of isolation and failure. Sarah came to understand that she was ignoring the source of her most acute discomfort, her personal life, and that she was seeking a solution—a job change—in the part of her life where she was actually the happiest and most successful. Just like the man under the streetlight, she was looking in the spot that was brightest. She'd been looking so intently that she "forgot" what she was actually searching for.

If your career or business feels like a disaster, and if everything you try to fix seems to make matters worse, you may be "streetlighting" yourself. One way to check for streetlighting is to ask yourself this question: *What is my goal?*

改

If you can't come up with a clear answer, consider that you have lost the ability to hear your own goals. It happens! But if you don't clearly know your goals, how will you know the steps to take to get there?

Here are some ways to clarify what you really want:

1. Make a detailed, specific list of what a fully successful life would look like for you. If this is easy and fun, like writing out a birthday wish list, you probably don't have a problem with streetlighting. But if you find the process difficult, producing vague answers, move on to the next item.

2. When you wake up in the morning, ask yourself, "What do I want from my personal life, my career, or my health?" (Yes, this is a business book. But the quickest route to clarity at work is to develop that same clarity for your life as whole.) Use a friendly, interested tone with yourself as you pose the question. Be patient as you await the answers.

3. As the answers come—and it may take weeks or even months—compile them into a list.

4. Once you have the list, spend just two or three seconds a day imagining that you've achieved all these

goals. Each week, add two or three more seconds and an additional practice session.

5. As you become more comfortable with this exercise, try a small step toward one of your goals. You may find yourself changing your habits without even trying.

BEFORE YOU BEGIN, A SMALL WORD

The members of Alcoholics Anonymous have a wise saying: "Life is simple, but not easy." As you take your business toward its first small step toward change, it can help to keep these words in mind. Even when *you* are eager to try kaizen, others in your organization may push you to change faster. They may want you to create change in the only way they understand: to buckle down, pull up your socks, and swing for the fences. Your own internal voice, conditioned by years living in a 70-millimeter Dolby world, may on occasion whisper: *Small is always slow. Big is necessarily better.* But small steps get you to the same place that big steps do; the main difference is that small steps are more likely to work. Sometimes they are faster, too.

So if your kaizen program is in danger of getting squeezed out by nagging and scolding voices, try this: upon rising in the morning, mark the first words and thoughts that come into your mind. When we are trying to change, many of us wake up to one of these common refrains:

You should have gotten up earlier!

Why did you eat so much last night?

Get out of bed—you should already be at your desk, and now look at the time!

Oh, no . . . another day of working hard to get nothing done!

改

You might also take note of what you're thinking as you take a shower, a place where many of us start mentally rummaging through the daily to-do list. In our haste to accomplish our goals, we easily lose touch with the gentleness that disarms our fears and allows us to calmly proceed with change.

Some of our haste to change and improve is based on the feeling that time is running out, both for our organizations and for ourselves. We get angry with ourselves, believing that we should have already achieved results or that we may not ever attain them. But kaizen is hopeful. It requires that we enjoy the journey, concentrating on mastery in the moment and trusting the rest to our brain and our spirit.

If you find yourself reciting your plans for improvement over and over with increasing panic, or if you hear an angry, abusive internal voice berating you for not being better, smarter, or more efficient, use those first moments of the day, upon awakening or in the shower, to ask a small question: "What am I grateful for *right now*?" Remember, all you have to do is make a habit of asking the question; the brain will eventually decide you are serious and will start preparing for tomorrow's question. Eventually, you'll soothe that ferocious critic who lives inside your head. And when that critic calms down, you'll find that you can bring your finest attitude and most productive intentions to the moments of your life—including the one you are living *right now*.

善

Appendix

REFLECTIONS ON KAIZEN

Inches make a champion.
—**VINCE LOMBARDI**

We chalked up a little success and then built on the momentum. You don't notice a snowball going down a hill until it grows to become the size of the stomach of a big, fat snowman. Within months, we saw small changes that eventually snowballed into a turnaround.
—**DAVID ABNEY**
President of UPS,
describing its effort to
expand into Europe

No matter how great your vision or strategy is, you have to get out there and be able to meet your customers' needs, one transaction at a time.
—**ROBERT NIBLOCK**
President of Loews Corporation

Nothing is particularly hard if you divide it into small jobs.
—**HENRY FORD**

There is a clear asymmetry between the scale of the problem and the scale of the solution. Big problem, small solution. Big problems are rarely solved with commensurately big solutions. Instead, they are most often solved by a sequence of small solutions, sometimes over weeks, sometimes over decades.
—**CHIP HEATH & DAN HEATH**
Authors of the book, *Switch*

改

Sustained success is largely a matter of focusing regularly on the right things and making a lot of uncelebrated little improvements every day.
—**THEODORE LEVITT, PhD**
Harvard Business School

Innovation doesn't arrive like a thunderbolt. It emerges incrementally, in bits and chugs, forged by a mixed bag of coworkers from up, down, and across the organization.
—**JACK WELCH**
Former CEO, General Electric

The secret of getting ahead is getting started. The secret to getting started is breaking your complex, overwhelming task into small, manageable tasks, and then starting on the first one.
—**MARK TWAIN**

Appendix

*If you do things incrementally, you have a
much better chance of succeeding.*

—MARTINA NAVRATILOVA

Won 167 Women's Single Tennis
Championships

*Do your little bit of good where you are; it's those little bits
of good put together that overwhelm the world.*

—DESMOND TUTU

善

167

NOTES

Chapter 1

1. Jim Collins, *Good to Great* (New York: HarperCollins, 2001).

Chapter 2

1. Tony Hsieh, "Happiness Matters: Creating a Culture for Business to Thrive," *Stanford Executive Briefings*, DVD, Kantola Productions, 2010, http://www.kantola.com/Tony-Hsieh -PDPD-380-S.aspx.

2. Jena McGregor, "USAA's Battle Plan," *BusinessWeek*, February 18, 2010, http://www .businessweek.com/magazine/content/10_09/ b4168040782858.htm.

Chapter 3

1. "What Drives Phenomenal Success?" *Stanford Executive Briefings*, DVD, Kantola Production, 2008, http://www.kantola.com/Colleen-Barrett -PDPD-142-S.aspx.

2. "LSE: When Performance-Related Pay Backfires," *Financial*, June 25, 2009, quoted in Daniel Pink, *Drive: The Surprising Truth About What Motivates Us* (New York: Riverhead Press, 2009).

3. Rosabeth Moss Kanter. *Confidence: How Winning Streaks & Losing Streaks Begin and End* (New York: Crown Publishing Group, 2006).

4. Gary Rivlin, "Who's Afraid of China? How Dell Became the World's Most Efficient Computer Maker," *New York Times*, December 19, 2004.

5. Joan Magretta, *What Management Is: How It Works and Why It's Everyone's Business* (New York: Free Press, 2002).

6. Jon Hilkevitch and Julie Johnsson, "Cost-Cutting Measures Fuels Debate at American Airlines," *Chicago Tribune*, June 27, 2010, http://articles.chicagotribune.com/2010-06-27/travel/ct -biz-0627-pilots-fuel-20100626_1_american-airlines-fuel-pilots -and-dispatchers.

7. Jane Brody, "A Basic Hospital To-Do List Saves Lives," *New York Times*, January 22, 2008, http://www.nytimes.com/2008/01/22/ health/22brod.html?_r=1.

8. David Welch, "Staying Paranoid at Toyota," *BusinessWeek*, July 2, 2007, http://www.businessweek.com/magazine/content/ 07_27/b4041060.htm.

9. Bryan Rooney, "UPS Figures Out the 'Right Way' To Save Money, Time, and Gas." *ABC News*, April 4, 2007, http://abcnews .go.com/WNT/story?id=3005890&page=1#.T7qLClKwV64.

10. Scott Simonson, "Employees of State Come Up with Ways to Ease Budget Woes," *Arizona Daily Star*, July 10, 2004.

11. Melanie Trottman, "Inside Southwest Airlines, Storied Culture Feels Strains," *Wall Street Journal*, July 11, 2003.

Chapter 4

1. Karl E. Weick and Kathleen M. Sutcliffe, *Managing the Unexpected: Resilient Performance in an Age of Uncertainty*, 2nd ed. (San Francisco: John Wiley & Sons, 2007).

2. Madan Birla, *FedEx Delivers: How the World's Leading Shipping Company Keeps Innovating and Outperforming the Competition* (New York: John Wiley & Sons, 2005).

3. Alan Mulally, interview by Charlie Rose, *Charlie Rose*, PBS, July 27, 2011.

4. David Lee Roth, *Crazy from the Heat* (New York: Hyperion, 1997).

5. Stephen J. Dubner and Steven D. Levitt, "The Odds of Surviving a Plane Crash," http://www.freakonomics.com/2010/08/20/the -odds-of-surviving-a-plane-crash/.

6. Gardiner Harris, "U.S. Inactions Let Look-alike Tubes Kill Patients," *New York Times*, August 20, 2010, http://www .nytimes.com/2010/08/21/health/policy/21tubes.html?_r=1& pagewanted=all.

7. Clay Chandler, "Full Speed Ahead," *Fortune*, February 7, 2005, http://money.cnn.com/magazines/fortune/fortune_archive/ 2005/02/07/8250430/index.htm.

8. Yves Morieux, "Smart Rules: Six Ways to Get People to Solve Problems without You," *Harvard Business Review*, September 2011: 78–86.

Chapter 5

1. Burkhard Bilger, "The Search for Sweet." *The New Yorker*, May 22, 2006: 40–46.

2. Joan Magretta, "Why Business Models Matter," *Harvard Business Review*, May 1, 2002: 87.

3. John Carlton Gallawa, *The Complete Microwave Oven Service Handbook: Operation, Maintenance, Troubleshooting, and Repair* (New York: Prentice-Hall, 2000).

4. Patrick Robertson, *Robertson's Book of Firsts: Who Did What for the First Time* (New York: Bloomsbury, 2001).

5. Patrick Robertson, *Robertson's Book of Firsts* (New York: Bloomsbury, 2001).

6. Susan Champlin, "Walt's Big Idea," *Alaska Airlines Magazine*, May 2005.

7. Merin, Jennifer, "SkyMall Has a Cure for Boredom: Shopping," *USA Today*, April 9, 2002, http://www.usatoday.com/money/ biztravel/bonus3/2002-04-09-skymall.htm.

8. Tom Kelley and Jonathan Littman, *The Art of Innovation: Lessons in Creativity from IDEO, America's Nation's Leading Design Firm* (New York: Doubleday, 2001).

9. Jon Gertner, "True Innovation," *New York Times*, February 26, 2012, http://www.nytimes.com/2012/02/26/opinion/sunday/innovation-and-the-bell-labs-miracle.html?_r=1&pagewanted=all.

10. Karl E. Weick and Kathleen M. Sutcliffe, *Managing the Unexpected: Resilient Performance in an Age of Complexity*, 2nd ed. (San Francisco: John Wiley & Sons, 2007).

11. Josh Quittner, "The Lessons of Amazon's Jeff Bezos," *Fortune*, May 5, 2008.

Chapter 6

1. Ian Robertson, *Mind Sculpture: Unlocking Your Brain's Untapped Potential* (New York: Fromm International Publishing Corporation, 2000).

2. Adam M. Grant, "How Customers Can Rally Your Troops: End Users Can Energize Your Workforce Far Better than Managers Can," *Harvard Business Review*, June 2011, http://hbr.org/2011/06/how-customers-can-rally-your-troops/ar/1.

3. Catherine Tinsley, Robin Dillon, and Peter Madsen. "How to Avoid Catastrophe," *Harvard Business Review*, April 2001, http://hbr.org/2011/04/how-to-avoid-catastrophe/ar/1.

4. Adi Ignatius, "The HBR Interview: We Had to Own Our Mistakes, An Interview with Howard Schultz," *Harvard Business Review*, July 2010, http://hbr.org/2010/07/the-hbr-interview-we-had-to-own-the-mistakes/ar/1.

5. Loizos Heracleous, Jochen Wirtz, and Nitin Pangarkar, *Flying High in a Competitive Industry: Cost-Effective Service Excellence at Singapore Airlines* (New York: McGraw-Hill, 2005).

6. Susan Chaplin, "Walt's Big Idea," *Alaska Airlines Magazine*, May 2005.

7. Jena McGregor, "Keeping Customers Happy," *BusinessWeek*, March 5, 2007.

8. M. Ellen Peebles, "Love Your Customers, A Conversation with Joe Girard," *Harvard Business Review*, July 2006, http://hbr.org/2006/07/love-your-customers/ar/1.

Chapter 7

1. Tony Schwartz and Catherine McCarthy, "Manage Your Energy, Not Your Time," *Harvard Business Review*, October 2007, http://leadershipdevelopment.iiwiki.edu.au/file/view/Manage+your+energy+not+your+Time+-+HBR.pdf.

2. Tara Parker-Pope, "To Keep Resolutions, Make Them Small," *Wall Street Journal*, December 31, 2002.

Chapter 8

1. David H. Freedman, "Why Scientific Studies Are So Often Wrong: The Streetlight Effect," *Discover Magazine*, July–August 2010, http://discovermagazine.com/2010/jul-aug/29-why-scientific-studies-often-wrong-streetlight-effect.

INDEX

改

善

改

善

改

Index

善